M000086130

About the Author

Hilary Bradt grew up in the Chilterns and trained as an occupational therapist, a profession she pursued in the USA and South Africa to finance her ever-longer periods of travel. Eventually the travel bug took over completely and, with her husband George, she spent four years backpacking through South America and Africa, founding Bradt Enterprises (now Bradt Travel Guides) along the way. She returned to England to concentrate on writing and publishing, punctuated by summers working as a tour leader. Her books include *Slow Devon and Exmoor* and 10 editions of the *Bradt guide to Madagascar*. She now lives in semi-retirement in Devon, dividing her time between writing, sculpting, and pottering around the county (http:// hilarybradt.com).

She was awarded an MBE in 2008.

Connemara Mollie

An Irish Journey on horseback

by Hilary Bradt

Bradt

First published in 2012 by
Bradt Travel Guides Ltd
IDC House, The Vale, Chalfont St Peter, Bucks SL9 9RZ, England
www.bradtguides.com

Published in the USA by The Globe Pequot Press Inc,
PO Box 480, Guilford, Connecticut 06437-0480

Text copyright © 2012 Hilary Bradt
Photographs copyright © 2012 Hilary Bradt
Illustrations copyright © 2012 Hilary Bradt
Map by David McCutcheon
Copy-edited by Shelagh Boyd
Text design and typesetting by Adrian McLaughlin
Cover design: illustration and concept by Neil Gower
              typesetting by Creative Design and Print.

ISBN: 978 1 84162 386 3

British Library Cataloguing in Publication Data
A catalogue record for this book is available from the British Library

Production managed by Jellyfish Print Solutions; printed in India

Acknowledgements

This book would never have been retrieved from the loft were it not for the encouragement
of Bradt's Rachel Fielding. A big thank you to her and also to Victoria Eveleigh and Deirdre
O'Sullivan who brought further encouragement along with knowledgeable feedback on
matters literary, horsey and Irish.

This book is dedicated to the wonderful people of western Ireland who provided conversation, food and accommodation for Mollie and me in 1984.

The Adventures of this Book

Why wait 27 years to publish a book? Here's why.

When I got home from my two-part Ireland adventure in 1984 I could hardly wait to start writing. Although I hadn't set out with the intention of writing a book, I'd kept a diary that I wrote up each evening in my tent, listening to my tape recorder play-back to catch the immediacy of the moment. But on my return I had books to publish and correspondence to catch up on, so it wasn't until the following spring when I found the opportunity to start my book. My parents went on holiday, leaving me to house-sit. I sat at the scrubbed kitchen table on which I had spent so many childhood hours drawing, painting and modelling horses, and started writing. I wrote in pencil on thick A4 pads of lined paper.

I worked steadily, checking my route on the maps I had carried with me, and listening again to the tape recorder to catch bits of dialogue, absorbing the cadences of the Irish accent and hearing the clip-clop of my horse's hooves as we covered the miles. When my parents returned three weeks later I had got it all down, but it needed a lot of revising and polishing, and for this I wanted another period of isolation away from my desk. A house-sitting opportunity came up again, this time in Haringey.

As well as solitude it had another advantage: an African grey parrot. I adore parrots.

I packed the two blue writing pads into a cardboard box, along with some maps and photos, put a few clothes into a suitcase, and drove my ancient car to north London, arriving at Julian's house at dusk. He had already left, but I let myself in and started unpacking the boot, putting the box containing the manuscript on the garden wall so I could take my case inside. There were lots of written instructions to absorb and a very cross parrot. The phone rang, Polly escaped and started walking determinedly down the stairs, and by the time I had got her back into her cage and found a sticky plaster for my finger where she'd bitten me, all I could think about was a nice cup of tea and then supper.

Next morning I cleared the table, cleared my mind, and prepared to start work on the book. But where the hell was the manuscript? It wasn't in my bedroom, nor in the kitchen. Nor, to my increasing dismay, in the car. As I traced my actions back to unloading the car, I felt that awful sinking feeling all too familiar to absent-minded people. I'd never picked the box up from the garden wall. And it was no longer there.

I was distraught. Remember, this was pre-computers, and the only copy of my precious book was the one I'd lost. I couldn't, wouldn't write it again. I cried for about an hour, and then found a sheet of white paper and a black marker pen. '£50 reward!' I headed it. Yes, a huge amount of money, but someone must have taken the box, been disappointed at the worthlessness of its contents, and could be persuaded to return it. I went to the photocopy shop and had 100 copies printed. These I put up on every telegraph pole and lamppost, and posted through all the neighbouring letterboxes for several blocks around. I was sure that someone would phone within a matter of hours, and certainly the next day, but I heard nothing. My despair deepened. I was alone in a strange house with a hostile parrot, and my whole purpose for being there had disappeared into thin air. Soon I had to leave not only London but England, being due to lead a trip to Peru where I would be out of communication for over a month.

Enter my knight in shining armour. Two knights. My friends Tanis and Martin Jordan heard about my loss – everyone I knew heard about my loss – and stepped in. "We'll find a dowser" said Tanis. "There's one who advertises in our local paper." I was easily convinced to leave it in their hands – I had run out of both time and options.

The Jordans contacted the dowser and visited him the day before I left for Peru. "Well, he was old and scruffy, maybe a gypsy," Tanis reported. "He had a pendant, some sort of crystal, and a grubby map of London. We found the house on Rokesly Avenue, and he dangled the pendant over the area and moved it slowly in all different directions. It started to go in a circle over a school, just at the end of that road. We watched. It was extraordinary – it just went round and round and he said 'That's where it is'. There were other possibilities that we circled on the map, then we paid him and off he went. My sister-in-law's going to help me with the search next week. I'll write to you in Lima."

I still have the letter.

"First, no luck so far. Ginny and I drove over to Hornsey, located the spot on the map and parked the car. The one thing I'd been dreading loomed in front of us – a builder's skip overflowing with rubbish. However, a quick check of the map showed it to be on the wrong road, plus the fact that it had probably only been there a few days made it an unlikely chance, we convinced ourselves, but we gave it a quick once-over just in case. We then located the exact spots on the map and these proved very interesting. One circle was over the school. The other was a long, shrub-lined drive leading to some barrack-style buildings. The sign at the end of the road said 'Rokesly Road Kitchens. No Entry'. So we went in. The place seemed perfect for our search, full of rubbish under wildly overgrown weeds etc. Of course, being an explorer, I'd failed to bring a stick to poke around with and was wearing flip-flops. A few nettle stings and one bee sting later I waded out of the jungle, found Ginny, and peered through the windows of the buildings which were locked and deserted. So that's still one possibility.

"After that we decided to knock on some doors. I think they thought we were selling something since most people seemed to be out. And when they did answer the door they couldn't understand what we wanted. But one lady not only believed us but was very helpful. She suggested the YMCA round the corner. The woman there was the most unhelpful person I've ever met. Her only comment was 'Have you any scientific evidence to back this up?' She did allow us to put a message on the notice board, though.

"We were having too much fun to stop, so worked our way back to where we'd started from, searching drains and gutters, and paid particular attention to the school. We now had long sticks so went round the perimeter pulling out rubbish and examining it (fortunately it was quite a clean school). It was closed for the holidays but where the circle on the map was, we peered through the windows and saw – kitchens! So maybe there's a link with those buildings we looked at earlier. We managed to find the caretaker – a large lady from Trinidad – who was the first really helpful person we met. She even knew what a dowser was. She insisted that we memorise the names of all the schools in the neighbourhood, including 'Tottenham High at de back of de church'.

"So I'll follow up with some phone calls tomorrow. And who knows. . .?"

I was sure that this exhaustive search would be rewarded, but when I returned home there was a message from Tanis saying they still had no news. Weeks passed, then months. I stopped thinking about the missing manuscript every day and came to terms with my loss. Sort of. I didn't want to write it all again so that was that.

Six months after I'd set that box upon the wall I was having dinner at my parent's house and the phone rang. "She's here if you want to speak to her," said my mother. "It's Julian," she whispered.

"There's a young man here with your manuscript," said Julian. "He wants to know if the reward is still on offer."

"What? How? When?" I spluttered. "I think it's better not to ask any questions," said Julian carefully.

So I got my manuscript back. And when I read it, after the six-month gap, I realised it needed a lot more than simple polishing. It needed a thorough revision. I put it in the loft and got on with other things. . .

Chapter 1

I t is noon in late May. The sky, washed by the rain of last night, is pale
greenish-blue, and joyful with the song of skylarks. The sun is warm on
my back. To my right, and a long way below, is the sea. The grassy track rises
gently between grey stone walls, disappearing into a dip between domed hills
which seem covered with silver-grey snow; for this is the Burren where the
limestone bones of the landscape break through the soil. And I am seeing
this view between the two grey ears of Mollie, my pony. My Connemara
pony. I am living a dream.

∩ ∩ ∩

It began with a book: *Four Rode Home* by Primrose Cumming. As a pony-
mad child I got through a horse book every week thanks to Harrods
Children's Library. This was an extraordinary service. Every Tuesday a smart
van would draw up in our drive, the front door would be pushed open and
a uniformed man would shout "'arrods!" and drop a brown-paper parcel on
the mat. Then he'd pick up the book I had hastily finished and wrapped that
morning. I would supply a list of all the titles I wanted to read and I was
very rarely disappointed. Only once, and I remember it vividly, they gave me

Little Women. I was so outraged that I've never been able to bring myself to read it. *Four Rode Home* was different from the usual story of the impoverished heroine acquiring a pony despite fearful odds and going on to win rosettes at the local gymkhana. Here the children trek through the English countryside from the New Forest to their home in Romney Marsh, staying in youth hostels and having lots of adventures. The idea was born: one day I would have my own pony and do a long-distance ride through changing scenery. And have lots of adventures.

My parents said bluntly that we couldn't afford a pony, had nowhere to keep one, and what about my asthma? They had a point; I was so allergic to horses as a young child that I had to take to my bed following each riding lesson. So I read about ponies, dreamed about ponies, galloped an imaginary pony along the grass verges along the bus route on the way to school, and drew them all over my rough book (for which I was punished). And each year I cut my birthday cake with my eyes tight shut and my wishes screaming to an unlistening fairy godmother.

By forcing my younger sister, Kate, to wish for a pony on her birthdays I doubled my chances, and finally our wishes half came true with Johnny. Johnny was the outgrown, evil-tempered first pony of a school friend who not only lived in a large house with rich parents, but had enviable curly red hair which she used to flatten down for Parents' Day with lacrosse grease. She'd also inherited their commercial sense. One day, in response to my endless pony drone, she said "You can hire Johnny for a week, if you like." The charge would be 10 shillings. Conveniently, Johnny was accustomed to being tethered, so where to keep him was not much of a problem; a neighbour gallantly said she didn't mind him mowing their back lawn for a week. Johnny was by no means a dream pony. He kicked. Not just a casual one-foot kick, but a full frontal attack with ears flattened and teeth bared, then wheeling around and letting fly with both heels. We loved him anyway, and since there was only one of him and two of us we were happy enough for him to stroll along the Buckinghamshire bridleways while one walked and the other rode. And we enjoyed the fringe aspects of pony care as much as the actual riding; grooming, picking out hooves, and cleaning tack each day like the children in the books. I wheezed and sneezed for a week, but at least I wasn't bedridden.

Now I was 11 or so I was considerably braver – reckless, even. Near our home was a smooth-surfaced private road which was perfect for roller skating. A group of ponies grazed in the adjacent field, and Kate and I used to sneak sugar lumps or carrots from the larder to feed to them in between bouts of wobbling along on our clip-on skates. One day I was sitting on the wooden fence while the pretty chestnut pony below me nuzzled Kate's hand for titbits. On impulse I lowered myself onto her back. I felt her muscles bunching under me and she took off at a gallop. A small part of me thought 'Wow, I've never been this fast!' and a much bigger part screamed 'Oh my God, she's going to jump that barbed wire fence!' At the last minute the pony braked and swerved. I fell off and, both unharmed, we stared at each other wide-eyed. I should have recognised an unbroken filly from the blonde tips to her mane and short tail.

Like Johnny, Ricky and Tara were not the stuff that dreams are made of, but the chance to look after them while their owner was in Canada came as one of the high spots of my childhood. No longer restricted to walking pace, Kate and I roamed the countryside, played silly games, entered and failed to win rosettes at gymkhanas, and fell off. It was easy to fall off both ponies, although in Tara's case it was always she herself who fell. This piebald mare, half carthorse with enormous hairy legs and a droopy lower lip, was so clumsy that if urged to a canter she periodically fell over. And she had a funny saddle. Her owner, Rosemary, told us proudly that it was an old army saddle that she'd lined with wool fabric from Daddy's factory. Heavy to carry and difficult to clean, we hated it. We hated Ricky's saddle too.

It was a 'felt pad' and we could feel his backbone through it. Little Ricky was only 12.2 hands high but could buck like a bronco and was so intelligent that keeping him became a battle of wits. He could get down on his knees and wriggle under the wire fence, leaving Tara neighing hysterically. Tara loved him and he repaid this affection by biting her at every opportunity. She would return from each ride with green slobber marks on her white bottom where Ricky had periodically grabbed a mouthful of grass then a mouthful of Tara.

When the sad time came to hand the ponies back I was 16 and suddenly grown so tall that at my last gymkhana it was I that knocked down the jump with my foot, not Ricky. But I'd learned a lot about pony care and found to my relief that my allergy to horses was diminishing with my increasing years.

After Ricky and Tara came Sonnet. When I left school at 17 I somehow persuaded my parents that they could now afford to buy us a horse. We'd earned the ponies' keep by working weekends at the local riding school which I was sure would continue to give us support. Besides, I said, I'd looked in *Horse and Hound* and a suitable animal need only cost about £70 (that was in 1958). Now that I fancied myself grown up, I wanted a horse not a pony, and I wanted one with all the qualities that Johnny, Ricky and Tara lacked: high head-carriage, keen, and a challenge to ride. 'Not novice ride' the advertisements would say, but these horses were still over £100. Then we were offered Sonnet. When she was led out of the stable I should have seen a 15.2hh bay mare with a too-large head, a ewe neck, a mean eye and sunken quarters. As it was I saw a proper horse with – joy-oh-joy – a normal saddle, and all for £70. We were assured that she was keen and not a novice ride and the horse-dealer confirmed that she'd do better out in a field all winter than in a stable where she might hot-up.

I rode her round the paddock and was thrilled to find that she was a comfortable ride, forward-going with smooth paces, and a nice high head.

I knew we were going to buy her. "We held a paper chase yesterday," the dealer said, "so she's had plenty of recent exercise."

"How did she do?"

"She bolted. But the man riding her was an idiot." I laughed sympathetically. It's such a shame when a lovely horse like Sonnet ends up with an idiot.

During the two years we had her, she bolted regularly. She charged through a hedge out hunting, she cantered through red traffic lights in our local town, and she jumped a motorbike plus rider that happened to be in the way during one headlong flight. The problem, we soon realised, was that this mare couldn't bear any pressure on her mouth from the bit. Sonnet's reaction to a pull on the reins was to throw her head up, breaking my glasses, and to increase her pace. We learned alternative ways of stopping, until one day the brakes failed.

There was a large field near our house where the wheat had been cut. I noticed that the gate had been left open and wanted to take Sonnet for a gallop there, an enclosed field providing a great opportunity to let her go for as long and as fast as she wanted. I decided to use her old rubber snaffle in this brief excursion since it was the bit she was most comfortable with. We never got to the field. Approaching one of our regular cantering places Sonnet, as usual, broke into a trot and started throwing her head around. When I restrained her I felt something break – it was the bit itself, the rubber having rotted – and the reins hung uselessly in my hands. Surprised at this unexpected freedom, she started to canter but leaning forward I managed to grab the noseband and slow her back to a trot. Then the noseband also broke and I was left with the bridle dangling uselessly from her neck. As she galloped off down the road I realised, sickeningly, that she was following the familiar route to her previous paddock, 2½ miles away. The country lane would soon join a major road which led steeply downhill, crossed the A313, and continued down to Chalfont St Giles below. By the time Sonnet reached the first junction she was galloping so fast that she skidded and nearly fell when making the turn. There were no cars coming, but I could see them ahead, lined up at the main road waiting for a gap in the traffic.

As Sonnet hurtled down the hill I could see a regular stream of cars on the main road and I knew that she would go straight across towards the village. I considered throwing myself off, then looked at the black tarmac whizzing past beneath her flying hooves and decided not to. Flying hooves resulted in flying shoes; they became loosened and I heard two of them sail off and land with a clink behind me. 'Damn,' I thought, 'those were new last week.' Then we reached the main road. The line of cars had diminished to one, and the driver must have looked in his rear-view mirror. He just had time to bump the car up onto the pavement as Sonnet careered past. I saw the cars moving steadily by on the main road; one passed just ahead of me, another behind me. Miraculously I was safely across and continuing on our headlong descent. The track leading to her old field was on the right, opposite the village pond, and I saw a black car pull over as this galloping apparition appeared in his mirror. But Sonnet was going too fast to negotiate the turn, hit the car with her shoulder and fell.

I lay on the ground until a very shocked-looking young man came and helped me up. I remember his white face and his trembling voice as he said "You alright, missy?" In fact I was. More or less. There was a crowd of people round Sonnet (being British, the onlookers were much more concerned with an injured horse than its shocked rider) who had a gaping wound in her shoulder, but at least she was on her feet with no broken bones. Someone gave me a cup of tea and a coin so I could phone home, tearfully explaining what had happened, and asking my ever-obliging parents to find a horsebox and a vet. I was just in time. A few minutes later an acquaintance rang my mother: "Ooh Mrs Cross, I've just seen your daughter galloping past our house on a runaway horse, so I was wondering if she's all right!"

I was uninjured apart from a chipped collarbone and the shock from which I never really recovered. My confidence was permanently affected and I no longer sought out difficult horses; I was happier on something quite docile and preferably small.

Chapter 2

"I travel, therefore I am." I don't know who said this, but what pretentious rubbish! Travel interests some people and not others, that's all. I travel because it happens to satisfy my curiosity and feed my various interests. And because I enjoy adventure which means travelling without fixed plans. And for this, nothing beats hitchhiking.

On a damp May morning in 1963 I set out with a friend to hitch from London to Dover and thence to the Middle East. At 21, Val and I had just completed our occupational therapy training and wanted a final fling before our first jobs. The couple who stopped for us a few miles from the ferry were from Peru. "Where's that?" I muttered to Val. "Africa, isn't it?" Well, geography was the first subject I gave up at school. Three months and £90 later I walked up the hill to my parents' house with a much better understanding of geography and politics. The lesson in frugality was long-lasting, but the real benefit was what I had learned about people. Hitchhiking teaches you that all over the world most people are astonishingly kind and generous, and even the dodgy ones can be dealt with diplomatically. And there's plenty of time for thought. Driving through eastern Turkey with two lecherous Cypriots I gazed at the unfenced hilly landscape laced with tracks trodden by laden donkeys and planned my long-distance ride. Some day, I told myself, I would buy a horse in the Russian Caucasus and ride it back to England through Turkey, Greece and Yugoslavia. Instead, I went to America, lured by the high salaries for OTs and proximity to Peru; I was now obsessed by the Incas.

While living in the United States I occasionally indulged my latent horsiness. Near Boston was 'Bob's Rent-A-Horse' where I rode an animal called Freeway which had a Sonnet-like tendency to bolt. At a fancier place in the Blue Hills the horses were stabled and full of oats, but you were still allowed out unaccompanied (inconceivable these days). Once, I fell off and spent the rest of my hour crawling around in the leaf litter looking for my glasses so I could be sure that I was catching a horse not a bush. Best of all was the week spent on a dude ranch in Wyoming. Here I learned to ride western style, wheeling my horse around with only one hand on the reins and spending all day on the many trails that led through the golden aspen forests and up into the foothills of Grand Teton. Hitherto I had only climbed mountains on foot and the advantage of doing it on someone else's legs was immediately obvious.

In 1969 I travelled to Peru in search of the Incas, found Machu Picchu, floated on a variety of vessels down the Amazon, and returned to England just in time for the NHS to treat my hepatitis. But I failed to settle down, went back to Boston and met George. He was an enthusiastic backpacker. No, he was an obsessive backpacker, spending three months every summer in some remote area of the US, hiking around on his own and carrying all his needs in a rucksack. I'd done some backpacking – indeed, I'd hiked 100 miles of the 2,000-mile-long Appalachian Trail – but tended to agree with some wag who said "Once you've seen two billion leaves you've seen them all". The eastern United States, I decided, had too many trees. To George I was an obsessive traveller, willing to abandon my job and friends and head off to such diverse places as Iceland and South America at the drop of a hat.

He'd done some travelling but considered there was no reason to leave God's Own Country which had the monopoly of beautiful scenery.

We compromised when we got married and planned to backpack round the world – with help from whatever vehicles were going our way. After four years, with half the globe still unexplored, we called a halt and started writing guidebooks. After all, no one else had described where to walk in South America and Africa. Nor, so publishers told us, did anyone want to read about such matters so we published the books ourselves.

∩ ∩ ∩

Writers learn as much from their books as their readers do. After a while you start to believe you've always known exactly what to pack for a ten-day trek in the Andes, where to go in Uganda, how to spot lemurs in Madagascar, what sort of boots to buy, how to make a tent, and so on. And you have a missionary-like zeal to spread the word. So not only did we publish books, we phoned a company called South American Wilderness Adventure and asked if they needed travel consultants. We were a bit vague about what we could do for them, but were sure that our boundless knowledge of the South American wilderness would prove useful in some way. The two affable Californians who ran the company were unimpressed at our consultancy idea but suggested that we become leaders. A similar offer had been made the previous year by the very charming director of an alarmingly up-market and expensive company offering luxury treks along Peru's Inca Trail. His clients were mostly male, said this elegantly dressed man with one gold earring, as he leaned back in his executive's chair, and they expected the utmost in comfort. The porters carried tables, chairs, chickens and wine. And if the clients wanted their feet massaged – well, that was the leader's job. He suggested we might like to lead one of his trips; his present leader, a young man, was often troubled by nocturnal visits from his clients and a friend thought a married couple might have an easier time. He told us how much he paid and we accepted the job with alacrity. Then we got down to details. "What," George wanted to know, "do we do if a client arrives for a trek with the wrong footwear?"

"You take him shopping for suitable boots."

"You mean to tell me it would be my job to drag some asshole around Lima looking for boots, when he's too stupid to come properly equipped?"

The letter arrived later that week: "Dear George, the fact that you referred to my beloved clients as assholes reinforces some doubts that I had. . ."

Wilderness Adventures seemed much more down to earth. We weren't expected to provide foot massages or night services, so with some hesitation we accepted their offer. I still regard this as an astonishing turn of events, having always felt myself to be a natural follower. How can someone be a leader if she's usually lost and if she's too cowardly to tell a waiter there's a caterpillar in the salad? Receptionists at hotels terrified me (not that I'd been in many hotels with receptionists) and I couldn't imagine arguing my way onto an overbooked plane or dealing with lost luggage.

While I was making the change from being a follower to a leader, George was also changing. The left-wing American hippie I'd married eight years earlier, discovered that all this while he'd been a closet capitalist and now he ran a publishing empire he could 'come out'. While I wanted to write, travel and lead trips, he wanted to stay home and run the business. While I believed that absence made the heart grow fonder, he thought otherwise and in 1980 the marriage ended.

∩ ∩ ∩

My dreams of doing a long-distance ride intensified. Now that I was alone, riding a wild Russian mare through Turkey no longer seemed such a good idea and my years away from Britain had nurtured nostalgic memories of heather-covered mountains and bridle paths through beech woods. I would buy a Highland pony and ride home to Bucks. Or perhaps a Welsh Cob and ride to Cornwall. Having neither the time nor the money to do such a self-indulgent trip didn't stop me thinking about it as I drove around the country selling books, or waited on a Peruvian hillside for the slower trekkers to catch me up. And it was in Peru that I moved a step closer. When planning the horse tour in my imagination, the question of what to bring and how to carry it had long been a sticking point. I knew I didn't want a packhorse; apart from the expense of buying or hiring two ponies, there would be the worry and inconvenience of controlling a second animal on the busy British roads and being limited to walking pace. I'd heard about people using small saddlebags and planning routes and night stops in advance, but that wasn't my style – I wanted to be completely flexible, to go or stop as the mood took me, or as the landscape and people invited me. This, after all, is what backpacking is all about and I felt that my experience as a walker could be put to good use; I knew that a rucksack containing all one's requirements for a wilderness trek of a week or more need weigh only 40lb. The question was how to carry that amount of luggage on a horse?

Then came the phone call. "Hi, Bill Roberson here. Do you want to join us on a horse trek in Peru? You know Tiki from Lima? She's running the thing but we haven't done this route before so we really need an extra helper." When I arrived at the trailhead in the Cordillera Blanca and saw the gear that Bill had brought from California I was thrilled. Instead of being carried in local-style hairy cow-hide nets suspended from wooden saddles, our heavy supplies were packed in smart panniers and our personal luggage was carried in saddlebags. "Put soft things such as clothes and sleeping bags in the middle section," said Bill, "and heavier things on each side. It's important to make sure that the two side bags are the same weight." He left us to get on with our packing but I was excitedly copying down the name of the manufacturer of this wonderful stuff: Morgans Horse Products. The saddlebags looked a bit like two large canvas handbags attached to each end of a duffle and were roomy enough to hold everything one would need for a lengthy solo trek. They were designed to fit over a western saddle but I thought they could probably be adapted for an English saddle, especially a military one like Tara's.

The first day was filled with drama. The previous evening, some boys had brought us two small owls they'd shot down with stones from their catapults. They wanted us to buy them for our dinner. Instead, we disinfected their wounds and put them on a nearby fence, hoping they'd recover enough to fly away during the night. One did, but on the morning of our planned departure the most severely injured of the two remained, eyes half shut but still alive and still with a small chance of survival, so we left it where it was. The muleteers arrived and started loading up their animals with much chatter and bursts of song. Suddenly there was silence. The headman walked slowly up to Tiki. "We can't go," he said simply.

"Why on earth not?"

"Don't you see?" he pointed to the little owl. "That means that someone will die on the trail." One of the men walked towards the bird with his machete, intending to kill it.

"Wait!" Tiki shouted. "It's only bad luck if you kill it, then someone will die. If you leave it alive everything will be all right." There was a long muttered discussion in the local Indian language, Quechua, before the men reluctantly agreed to continue.

We started our ascent towards the shining white peak at the head of the valley, the line of packhorses making their sure-footed way along the narrow trail cut into the side of the mountain. Suddenly, behind me, I heard a noise like a police siren. One of the elderly women clients was clutching the pommel of her saddle, looking down at the river a few hundred feet below, and screaming. Her *arriero* stared at her in astonishment, his hand on the reins of the stationary horse. He spoke no English but could understand the

"No!" that she fitted in between screams. We also stared. If she had a fear of heights, someone suggested, perhaps she should dismount and walk. She did, and the screams only got louder.

Bill told her they'd better have a little chat. The path got considerably worse later on in the trek and if vertigo was such a problem she was in for a bad time. So were the rest of the group. "I didn't know," she sobbed, "I prepared for the trip by riding in the woods. I was fine there." It looked as though we'd have to turn back. This suggestion, however, activated her husband, who up till that time had been gazing at the scenery. "For Christ's sake, Martha, get a grip!" And to our amazement and her great credit, she did. Occasionally faced with a precipitous drop, her grip loosened and some screams escaped, but she learned to shut her eyes and allow her *arriero* to lead the horse. He was very kind: "*Venga, venga abuelita*," he murmured soothingly as he patted her knee. 'Come, come little grandmother.'

I learned a lot about horses' capabilities during this trek. In England I'd never have dreamed of asking a horse to climb steps roughly hewn from rock, to ford fast rivers over slippery boulders, or climb a pass of 15,000 feet. Not, come to think of it, that there's much opportunity of tackling such terrain in Britain. And as well as finding out what horses can do, I learned what we can do for them in return. Less-developed countries are not known for their kindness to animals, but our Peruvian muleteers made sure that the horses, donkeys and mules had adequate grazing each night and an hour's break without their loads in the middle of the day. This consideration was balanced by their disturbing custom of cutting off a sick donkey's ear to allow the disease to run out, and shoeing a nervous horse by throwing it on its side, tying the unwanted legs together and banging the shoe on each outstretched hoof in turn, while an assistant distracted the animal with a cord twisted around its upper lip.

∩ ∩ ∩

This wasn't my first experience of horse management in the third world. George and I had hired two ponies in Ethiopia to transport us into the Simien Mountains. One was a pack animal and we were to take turns in riding the other. George had only been on a horse a couple of times before, so was more than willing to accept the guiding hand of Ephram, the owner. I, however, waved him away airily in the knowledge that with my experience of both English and western styles of riding I could control any horse. Not this one, I couldn't. It walked briskly off in the wrong direction while I tried everything in my repertoire to turn it around. Hauling on one rein had no effect, nor did neck reining. Humiliated, I had to accept help. It wasn't until I watched an Ethiopian steer his mule that I learned how the locals do it: whack the animal on the side of the face with a stick. It soon learns to turn sharply in the opposite direction at the mere glimpse of the whip.

Coming down the steep mountain trails where the path is made of boulders and deep mud, the Ethiopians didn't bother with steering. We always got off and walked these sections, not trusting ourselves to stay in a lurching saddle angled at 45 degrees. The Ethiopians just swung themselves back to front, gripping the high cantle of the saddle while the mule (valued well above horses) picked its own way down the slope.

Ephram demonstrated other local methods of horse management, though with no common language our miming abilities were put to the test. Most evenings, as we pitched our tent and cooked our dinner, he'd hobble the ponies by tying their heads to a foreleg – an effective and not unkind method that allowed them to graze with unrestricted movement but prevented them from throwing up their heads and galloping off. One evening I'd set up the tent and came to tell George that supper was ready, and I found him hopping on one leg in front of Ephram, the other leg hooked over an arm, while he pulled his head towards his knee. Ephram understood this extraordinary display much faster than I did. George was reminding him to hobble the ponies. The Ethiopian did his 'It's alright, don't worry' gesture (which he had come to use frequently) so we left him chewing his way through that day's ration of *injera* (Ethiopian bread resembling grey foam rubber) and went to our tent. Early the next morning George, up early as usual, came to tell me something was dreadfully wrong with the ponies. I crawled out of my sleeping bag and followed him a short way from the campsite to where they were both lying stretched out on the grass looking faint. Anxiously, I urged them to their feet; they were not sick but were dead lame. I interrupted Ephram's breakfast of more grey foam rubber and insisted he came with me. When I pointed out the ponies staggering around on three legs he gestured 'It's all right, don't worry'. I gasped when he produced a knife, wondering what gruesome demonstration of Ethiopian surgery we were about to witness. Within seconds of taking hold of a limp foreleg, he held up the source of the problem: a thin piece of cord tied tightly round the animal's leg just below the knee. The other horse was released from its 'hobble' the same way. He smiled at our consternation and shrugged off our anger. 'After all,' he was probably saying, 'it works!' Sure enough, by the time we were ready to leave the horses were sound again, but he never again used that method of restraining them during the night.

∩ ∩ ∩

After the Peru trip I wrote to Morgan's for a catalogue. My plans took shape around the pictures of horses and riders fully prepared to spend several days or weeks in the wilderness, and I knew I would be able to do my ride. All that remained was when and where, and, to some people, why? Was I going to make it a feat? To ride from John O'Groats to Land's End, for instance? The answer was emphatically no. I've always disliked the publicity given to travellers who set out to beat some sort of record. For me it's the travel itself that is sufficient, the opportunity to see beautiful scenery, observe wildlife and, when I could get up the courage, meet new people; that was my Achilles heel as a traveller – I was shy and it always took an effort to talk to new people. So travelling alone, I was not at all afraid of any physical risk but the need to make contact with strangers was always an anxiety.

I couldn't decide where to go. I was ashamed to admit it, but I wasn't brave enough to do a solo horse trip in the developing world. There were just too many challenges, and the end of my marriage to feisty George had left me more shaken than I wanted to acknowledge. I still fancied Britain, with a nod at T S Eliot's lines: "We shall not cease from exploration. And the end of all our exploring will be to return to where we started from and know the place for the first time." But I hadn't come to the end of all my exploring. . .

I know, Iceland! It had all the requirements: lovely scenery, a tough breed of native pony and friendly people who generally spoke English. I'd been there and loved it. I tried out the idea by rather casually mentioning in my Christmas letter that I was going to buy a native pony in Iceland and do a long-distance ride. I received a reply from a horsey friend: "Ireland! What a great idea. A Connemara pony would be strong enough and it's such a beautiful country. And they love horses." Oh. My handwriting. . . well, let's think about Ireland then. It had never come into my reckoning, perhaps because of a very wet family holiday there when we children had sulkily squelched up Ireland's highest mountain in mist and rain. All I could remember was sinking into bog up to the top of my thigh, and weeping with the misery of it all, while my father retrieved my missing plimsoll from the black, watery depths. But now, suddenly, everything fell into place. Ireland was an ideal choice. Scenic, safe, English-speaking. . . perfect!

I still didn't know *when* I would do my ride since I couldn't imagine ever having enough money. I needed enough capital to buy a pony. This, I thought, would be the only way to do the ride cheaply. I could sell the animal at the end of the trip and since it would, if all went well, be a fitter and more worldly-wise pony by then, there was no reason why I shouldn't sell at a profit. Hiring would be expensive and would force me to do a circular tour. Apart from the lack of money, there were other considerations that made me wonder if I was really ready for this. It was several years since I'd even been on a horse and nearly 25 years had passed since we'd sold Sonnet. It all became a bit overwhelming.

Then came a bit of Peruvian serendipity which served as a dress rehearsal. In 1983, when leading one of my Andean treks, I had to evacuate a sick client. Lynn wasn't dangerously ill, but she had acute mountain sickness caused by the thin air of the Andes and needed to get down to a lower altitude. Fortunately I had a co-leader (a new recruit who was learning the ropes) so was able to leave him in charge while an *arriero* and I escorted Lynn on horseback down to the valley and a bus to Cusco. At that point she was feeling so much better I discussed with Faustino the possibility of my rejoining the group. They were an exceptionally nice bunch of people, the scenery was superlative and the weather fine. Peter, my co-leader, and the group could have managed without me but I wasn't sure that I could manage without them. Lynn encouraged this plan. She was happy to take the bus to Cusco and spend a few days on her own before we rejoined her.

Faustino agreed to rent me a horse so that we could ride together and intercept the group. If we left early, he said, the trip could be done in two days. At 6.30 the next morning he had introduced me to Sambo, a scrawny black pony of 14 hands or so. My luggage was in two flour sacks tied each side of the saddle, but what drew my eye was Sambo's head collar. Made from strong leather decorated with silver rivets, it looked practical as well as versatile. Not so the saddle, which was old and poorly padded, with stirrups of unequal length. I mounted and followed Faustino as we trotted briskly through the village. We trotted briskly towards the mountains, and we trotted briskly to the settlement that marked the trail head. I begged Faustino to slacken his pace and let me go on foot for a while. I could barely stand up. My thighs were rubbed raw, my knees felt as though six-inch nails had been driven through them, and my bottom was pulverised.

Faustino had told me he would find us lodging for the night on the way to the high pass, so when we came to natural hot springs I told him that I was going to have a bath. He settled down to watch with interest.

In a high valley surrounded by snow peaks, a one-room hovel stood alone under the white bulk of Mount Ausangate. This was our shelter for the night, the home of an alpaca farmer and his daughter. We were given a shy welcome and while Faustino caught up on gossip, I climbed a nearby hill to watch the setting sun give a golden outline to the woolly alpacas.

Returning to the *casita* in the failing light I ducked under the low door and groped my way to a seat in the corner covered by a sheepskin. It was surprisingly comfortable. The girl handed me a plate of tiny boiled potatoes, to which I added cheese brought from the town. When darkness came at 6.30 we prepared for sleep. The girl watched enthralled as I blew up my air mattress, stuffed a T-shirt with a sweater to make a pillow, and pulled my sleeping bag out of its stuff bag. Faustino, who spoke Quechua, relished his role as man of the world and explained the use of each item, but when she saw me climb into the blue cocoon sleeping bag, it was too much for her – she burst into giggles and little explosions of laughter accompanied the rest of my preparations. When she was ready for sleep she just curled up on a pile of sheepskins.

Faustino and the girl got up at 4.30 to round up the horses and start the cooking fire, fuelled with llama dung which was white with frost. I shivered in my blue cocoon until it was light enough to see my surroundings. That was when I discovered that the chair I'd reclined on the previous evening was in fact half a sheep carcass with a well-sprung rib cage.

We set off at sunrise and headed for the pass. I led Sambo and we both gasped for breath as we toiled our way upwards. At 16,000 feet every step is an effort, but the view from the top – a broken semi-circle of snow-covered peaks with a whipped-cream glacier below us – was breathtaking in the best sense of the word. And after that it was downhill all the way to my rendezvous with the group.

Back in Cusco I bought a head collar just like Sambo's. I had taken the first step.

Chapter 3

I put in my order to Morgans: saddlebag, nosebag and a single-stake hobble. In the absence of any advice, I'd given the subject of tethers and hobbles a lot of thought; it was fortunate that I'd seen so many varieties of horse restraints while travelling abroad since the English seem to have a blind spot on the matter. The horsey people I spoke to were shocked even at the idea of a nosebag, let alone something as gypsy-like as a tether or hobble. They were not much more helpful over gear for me. Since I hadn't been to a saddler selling riding clothes for about 20 years, I browsed through a smart shop in London. It seemed that nothing had changed since I was a teenager; there was no innovative, lightweight rain gear, no saddlebags and certainly no hobbles or tethers. The horse's comfort was catered for but not the rider's; appearance was put before utility, echoing the Pony Club dictum that 'the rider should always be smartly turned out'.

There was no illustration of how to use the single-stake hobble I was purchasing, but I assumed it was actually a form of tether, tying the horse by a leg rather than by the neck, which seemed a good idea. Horses' necks are designed for pulling, but not so their slender legs, so I assumed that a leg tether need not be as strong. We had tethered Johnny from a neck strap, using a chain and a heavy iron spike to drive into the ground with an equally heavy hammer. For this trip I had to reduce the weight wherever possible, so bought a nylon rope instead of a chain, and in a camping catalogue I found a light aluminium dog-tether which looked like a giant corkscrew and was almost impossible to pull out of the ground using brute force.

It was much easier visualising the horse's night-time arrangements than my own. I was planning to camp, which was fine. What was not fine was that I would have to ask permission to camp in farmers' fields and that brought up the spectre of 'batey' farmers. Kate and I, like most children raised in the country, had done our share of trespassing. Every now and then we were caught and roared at by the farmer. The conditioned reflex was so enduring that even in adulthood a glimpse of the landowner while mushrooming would send me quivering behind a bush, and cause me to turn back and quietly retrace my steps rather than follow a public footpath through a farmyard. So the thought of having to ride a horse up to a farmhouse each evening to ask for a field was dreadful. I mentioned this anxiety to an aristocratic Irish acquaintance. Suppose I trespassed without realising it? "Oh there's nothing to worry about," said Kieran, "they might threaten you with a shotgun, but they'd never hurt you." I was not reassured. Danger is part and parcel of adventurous travel, and there's something almost refreshing about rational fear; it's irrational fear that's so debilitating because of the feeling of foolishness that goes with it. It is hard to admit that someone who has survived detention in Uganda, with her nerves intact, quails at the thought of making a phone call, entering a crowded room or ringing a doorbell.

When I was married to George it was easy. He had no social fears and, in his company, nor had I. Now I was alone I wanted to learn to like being alone. To travel with a companion would have been a cop-out. My Connemara pony, I reckoned, would provide the company I needed.

As well as my conscious worries about farmers I had a variety of subconscious anxieties that surfaced in a rich crop of dreams. Many of them had elements of realism, as in the one where I had just bought a horse and had pitched my tent in a busy campsite. The field was full of tents, spaced as neatly and regularly as war cemetery crosses. Through this order my disorderly horse wandered, crawling into other people's tents and making a thorough nuisance of itself. I decided I must tether it with the new hobble. It was only after I bent down to attach the strap to its leg that I realised, to my horror, that I hadn't inspected all of the horse when I bought it. It was a fine looking animal – from the body up – but its legs were as tiny and slender as a sheep's. No way could it carry me and the luggage.

Another dream had me wandering in a maze of urban alleyways, and I was angry with my horse for sneaking up to the back doors of the houses and ringing the doorbell. Then I saw, walking across a field, a well-dressed man in a suit with a copy of the *New Yorker* magazine sticking out of his breast pocket. I asked my horse if it subscribed to the *New Yorker*; if so, perhaps we could share a copy? To which the horse replied, "I'm a *Daily Express* man myself."

I set a date. In 1983 I was offered four trips to lead, which would give me enough money to buy a horse in 1984. I was determined to set out at the end of April. By March I had most of my equipment laid out in my sister's house where I was living, and a rough idea of what I wanted to do. Since I planned to buy a Connemara pony it was logical to start in Connemara, which I learned was not a county but a region – a fat peninsula, really – in the west of Ireland encompassing most of Co Galway. But I still lacked the most important piece of equipment – a saddle. I thought longingly of Tara's military saddle and remembered ruefully how much we had hated it. Perhaps I could advertise for one in *Horse and Hound*? Then Kate mentioned casually that one of the other mums she chatted up outside the school had told her she had a saddle in the attic and didn't know what to do with it. It had been given to her husband by a landowner to 'get rid of' but they knew nothing about horses nor how to go about selling such a thing. Kate went to have a look. "It's a funny sort of saddle. A bit like Tara's. But it looks OK." I phoned Jenny and arranged to come over. Propped up in the corner of her conservatory was a brand new military saddle! I couldn't believe it. Designed for long journeys, its deep seat and high arch made it comfortable for both horse and rider. The suede knee rolls on the saddle flaps would add to my comfort and the plentiful supply of D rings on the extensions at the back meant secure attachment for the saddlebags. I was euphoric at this find. Neither Jenny nor I had any notion how much a saddle like this was worth, but she was happy with the £50 I offered. I took it home, saddled the back of my armchair, and gloated. Bored friends were brought to see it and I couldn't resist stroking it whenever I passed. I took my acquisition of such a fine saddle to be a sign that God was on my side.

Kate was a good antidote to all this gushing optimism.

"You think this trip will be fun?" she responded to some casual remark of mine. "You'll wake up to hear drip drip drip on the tent roof. You'll pack up in the rain, ride 10 miles in the wrong direction and it'll still be raining when you pitch camp. You'll be trotting along and there'll be 'clip-clop squidge clop' and you'll realise the horse has lost a shoe. You'll ask where the nearest farrier lives and they'll tell you 'We don't have one. There wasn't the demand, you know'. You'll be lying in your sodden tent and you'll hear," – and she did a passable imitation of a horse coughing – "outside. Or you'll go to catch it in the morning and find it lying down looking ill. Or lame. . . I wonder how you'll get rid of it for insurance purposes. . . push it over the cliffs or under a double-decker, I suppose."

Kate had actually raised some points I had decided not to think about too much. What would I do if the horse went lame or became ill? I didn't know but wrote 'insurance' on my list of things to do when once I'd bought a pony, since I couldn't insure a non-existent animal. I knew shoeing would be a problem, but there was nothing much I could do there except contact local riding schools to find out which farrier they used; and as for getting lost, this was inevitable since I'm devoid of any sense of direction. I can't even find my way out of a house (usually opening the broom cupboard door as I say goodbye over my shoulder) let alone a town. I need a distinctive landmark, like a mountain range which I hoped I'd find in Ireland. And I know how to use a compass.

I was impressed with what I'd accomplished by the end of April. It had been the usual effort to get all my publishing work up to date and organised for my assistant to take over. A week before departure I needed one final piece of equipment. "What's that you're making?" asked six-year-old Nicholas as I sat sewing.

"It's a bag to carry everything I need during the day when I'm riding."

"Oh yes, I know, like perfume and cheese-and-chutney rolls." Just so.

I also had to adapt the saddlebags to fit my new saddle and it seemed a good idea to try everything on something a little more horse-shaped than my armchair. An acquaintance was willing to lend her pony as a tailor's dummy and I was relieved to find my design for the cheese-'n'-chutney-roll bag was perfect to attach to the D-rings in front of the saddle and could quickly be detached to carry as a handbag. The big saddlebags seemed all right, though I'd need to add some extra straps and an additional girth to prevent them bouncing up and down when I trotted. The final adjustment would have to be made after I bought a pony. And that was the one item still missing.

I had no idea how to look for a pony in Ireland (remember, this was long before the internet). I didn't know if there was an equivalent to *Horse and Hound*, with its pages of advertisements of horses for sale, and anyway I wanted to buy a Connemara pony in Connemara, which limited the search. At least I had a friend in Dublin: Dorothy, who had shared the ill-fated

Lynn's tent in Peru. Her cousin, John Daly, happened to be one of the best-known breeders of Connemara ponies and show jumpers in Ireland. Then there was Kieran who had once hired horses from a chap called Willie Leahy in Loughrea. "Try Willie," Kieran said. "Sorry I can't help," said John Daly, "but try Willie Leahy, and come and visit me when you're underway." So I wrote to Willie Leahy, found Loughrea on the map, not far from Galway, and knew that here at least was a likely source of good, strong ponies since Willie also organised horse treks.

My equipment was complete. For tack I had the saddle and girth, a snaffle bit and reins, plus little straps to attach it to my silver-studded Peruvian head collar, and an Ecuadorian sheepskin to guard against saddle sores. Then there were the two saddlebags (the small cheese-'n'-chutney-roll one for the front and the capacious American one behind), the tether rope ending in a strong clip, a nylon dog lead for leading the pony or tying up for brief periods, the hobble and corkscrew picket, a nosebag and a plastic collapsible bucket. That took care of the horse. I was equipped as for backpacking, with a rain cape designed for cyclists, waterproof chaps which I could put on over my hiking boots, a tiny 'Peapod' tent, ThermaRest mattress and a light sleeping bag, a water flask (which clipped to the saddle D rings, along with the tether rope), maps, books, compass, camera, binoculars, a change of clothing, and all the other things needed for safety, comfort and enjoyment, including a small transistor radio. Altogether it weighed about 50lb.

I'd give so much thought to what to bring and how the horse would carry it, I'd forgotten to consider how I myself would carry it to Ireland. I'd chosen to book a coach and ferry because the luggage is loaded on in London and doesn't have to be touched again until the coach arrives in Dublin. Or so I thought. But I still had to get it to the coach. Kate took me to the local train station in the afternoon of April 26th where three people were needed to load the five bags onto the train. And these weren't bags in the normal traveller's sense of the word, these were five plastic bin liners, supposedly extra strong but already starting to split.

Since the coach left Gloucester Road at 8am I thought it provident to spend the night with friends in London, even though it meant bringing all my luggage to Clapham. As the taxi driver helped me out at the aptly named Shamrock Road address, I thought I should explain this abundance of oddly shaped bags. "So you're goin' to be 'orsin' around in Ireland, are you? Well, that's summink, I suppose!"

Chapter 4

"Dear Kate," I wrote from Dublin. "No, I haven't got a horse, I've got luggage." The sheer awfulness of getting all those bags to Dublin and then to Galway pushed all other thoughts from my mind. The plan had been so sensible: book a coach direct from London to Dublin so I wouldn't have to carry my uncarryable luggage. The coach, I assumed, went onto the ferry. Not so, it turned out. The coach dropped us on the dock at Holyhead, seemingly miles from the boat, and we were told to remove all our luggage. Another coach would meet us on the other side, so they said. Of course there were no trolleys to be seen, but since I couldn't physically carry all my stuff I managed to find one lurking in some dark recess and was just piling my luggage on when an officious man appeared and said, "You're doing it all wrong." He took all my things off and loaded the trolley with cases belonging to a girl standing next to me. Then came my oddly shaped and already splitting plastic bags. The girl was most grateful and I was not particularly gracious as I pushed the thing towards the mass of people waiting to board the boat. Then, of course, I wasn't allowed to take the trolley onto the boat so I had to heave my stuff on board in relays, banging the backs of people's knees as I went. Some turned round to remonstrate but after a look at my furious face, changed their minds. I just left it all in a pile near the gangway.

At least the sea was calm, and so was I until I had to get the luggage off the boat and into the next coach. Fortunately someone helped me this time, but my troubles weren't over. Dun Laoghaire, Dublin's port, is so near the city they hadn't bothered to provide a proper coach. This one had no luggage compartment. I struggled inside with my five bags, clunking people on the head with the saddle, which was starting to emerge from its torn plastic bag, and swearing instead of apologising. After a short while the bus stopped by what looked like a bombsite and everyone got out. Or rather, most people got out. I didn't. After we were underway I learned from the driver that this was the only stop in Dublin (the bus was continuing to some other town) so he had to make a special stop while I heaved and clonked and swore my luggage down the aisle and traffic piled up behind.

I did manage to flag down a taxi, however, and had a lovely warm welcome from Dorothy. Then the whole process had to be repeated next day when I took another bus to Galway, except that there was no question of getting a trolley to take the bags 'five minutes' from the bus stop to the nearest left-luggage place in Galway station. It took me a good 20 minutes, again working in relays and just hoping no one would investigate the pile of bulky plastic bags apparently abandoned by the bus stop (in London, at that time, the area would have been cordoned off and a controlled explosion would have taken place – Galway was less IRA conscious). By that time I was so exhausted I just checked into the first B&B I could find. Serious horse-hunting would begin tomorrow.

I had a list of telephone numbers and stood in a Galway phone box, steeling myself to call these possible horse-dealers one by one. I'd already made an appointment to see Willie Leahy in Loughrea, but there were several other recommendations which I knew I should check out.

None could help. The last one was Lady Someone who, I'd been told, knew all about Connemara ponies. I'd found two listings in the phone book, one for Lord Someone and the other *The* Lord Someone. 'Lord' without the definite article sounded marginally less frightening so, quaking, I tried that number. Then to the question "Who shall I say is phoning?" I had to go into a bumbling explanation of who I was and what I wanted. Her Ladyship was very nice but terribly busy with the trustees so couldn't really help. And that was enough. I'd made an effort to broaden my search, but it all came down to Willie Leahy.

Willie had made it clear on the phone that there was no point in my heading out to Loughrea until later in the week. All his ponies were out at grass, but he would be bringing them in soon to prepare for the first trek of the year which was heading out on Monday. Could I come on Thursday, when he should have something to show me? It was Tuesday, and I didn't want to fritter my time away in Galway, so thought I'd take a look at the Aran Islands, or at least the largest one, Inishmore.

It was such a beautiful morning that I decided to walk the five miles to the ferry, rather than take the bus. The landscape was an appetiser for the Connemara countryside that was to come: dry-stone walls, thatched cottages and fields full of flowers. Everyone said "hello" and at every step I felt better about travelling alone.

I'd expected Aran to be touristy, but far from it. On arrival, visitors had to climb up a vertical metal ladder to reach the pier. The Americans on the boat could hardly believe it. Lots of "Oh my"s. Then we had the choice of jaunting car, bike or foot to get around; I chose the latter because I thought I'd see more. It was still a cloudless day and I walked along a narrow lane with tiny fields enclosed in stone walls and absolutely choc-a-bloc with wild flowers: primroses, celandine, cowslips, violets, and several I didn't know including lots of lovely purple-coloured orchids. When I came across the first one I was hugely excited, thinking I'd found something very rare since it was so pretty.

Then I saw fields full of them and realised that these early purple orchids are to the west of Ireland what dandelions are at home.

I ate my lunch on a natural rock bench overlooking a rock-and-sand bay. There was no-one around. Then I cut up through the fields, climbing all those wobbly stone walls to the upper road where I hoped to find a B&B. The first village was deserted, but as I walked on to the next one I fell in with an old fellow in a peaked cap who was quite talkative. I was relieved that I could understand him; most of the local folk who I'd overheard chatting to each other were speaking Irish. "The sweaters? You won't find people knitting them by hand these days. They have knitting machines. And the wool comes from the mainland. Not many sheep here any more." We walked on in silence for a while. I ventured something about the lovely weather. "'Tis awful dry. Not right for the time of year." I didn't share his gloom about the unremitting sunshine until Mrs O'Flaherty at the B&B told me I couldn't take a bath because of the water restrictions.

She showed me the route to the most important historic site on the islands, Dun Aengus, a prehistoric (1st-century AD) stone ring right at the edge of a 270-foot cliff. The fortress itself is very fine and the location stupendous. I walked along the cliff edge in the late afternoon sunshine and marvelled. The cliff is not just sheer, it's Shakespearean sheer, seeming to 'o'er hang and jutty his confounded base, swilled with the wild and wasteful ocean'. The wild and wasteful ocean is eating into the confounded base so dramatically that sooner or later it's all going to fall into the sea. Meanwhile there are clumps of pink thrift and other flowers, and geometric-shaped slabs of limestone looking hand-laid and levelled, with rectangular chasms going down to bottomless depths, and lots of noisy sea birds. I was entranced and walked for miles before realising that it was nearly nightfall.

It was 10 o'clock before I got back to the B&B so Mrs O'Flaherty was naturally worried, but after I'd apologised we settled down to a cosy hour by the fire watching a TV programme on the new Northern Ireland Forum. It was my first introduction to The Troubles from a local viewpoint. When I was talking about my proposed trip in England, some people were surprised that I would venture to 'such a dangerous country'. Hard to imagine now, but in 1984, only five years after Lord Mountbatten was assassinated by the IRA in Co Sligo, that was not an unusual opinion. However, I never met anyone in the Republic who had any sympathy for the IRA or who considered unity a reasonable goal, although I wrote in my diary that 'even after a week of talking to people and reading Irish history I feel that Irish unity is the most moral goal. Whether it can ever, or should ever, be achieved is another matter'.

"Isn't he good-looking, God bless him," Mrs O'Flaherty said, pointing at the screen.

"Who is he?"

She looked at me sharply. "The Taoiseach!" I still didn't understand but kept quiet; clearly I had a way to go before I could safely discuss Irish politics.

I'd arranged to meet Willie Leahy that morning in Loughrea. He met me off the bus and I explained my plans over a glass of Guinness, before heading out in the drizzle to look at some horses. Only look, mind you, they were loose in a huge field, and Willie said that catching them was not an option. Not until the weekend, anyway. Nor could I get any idea from him about how much a suitable pony might cost. It was all very frustrating. I spent the night in an icy B&B with no hot water (I'd taken the precaution of bringing my toothbrush and purse, knowing I'd probably miss the last bus back to Galway) and looked at more loose horses, and more rain, the next day. The experience was conclusive in one sense – I decided that without my own transport I was pretty much stuck in Loughrea, and since Willie had lots of horses and seemed willing to sell me one – eventually – I might as well collect my luggage and camp nearby until he was ready to do business. Eva, his assistant, assured me that with a trek starting on Monday, he would have to bring in the horses the following day.

I'd been dreading another tussle with the luggage, but for once luck was on my side. The bus left from just outside the station, where I'd stored my stuff, and had a spacious baggage compartment at the back. Eva was there to meet me, as promised, and after dumping my things we went straight to the field to help in the roundup. And roundup is the right word – the scene bore more resemblance to Texas than the British Isles. There were horses galloping in all directions pursued by whooping boys on horseback, sheep scattering, dogs barking, people shouting conflicting instructions and a happy air of confusion and chaos. Finally, as dusk came, the excited horses were all penned in a corral so the ones needed for the trek could be caught and loaded onto the waiting horsebox. Even this wasn't easy in the failing light with thirty or so horses milling around and occasionally making unsuccessful breaks for freedom. I kept an eye on the two grey mares that Eva had picked out for me, to make sure they were included in the selection. One was a very pretty dark dapple grey with a small head and slender legs – typical of the lighter build of Connemara pony that is popular now. The other was also Connemara but the old-fashioned type: heavier, stronger, not so elegant and with hairy fetlocks like Tara's. But I'd admired her general bearing and action as she trotted round the field with her head held high and long mane and tail flowing. I was glad they were both grey (the heavier one was almost white); apart from being photogenic it made for good visibility in poor light conditions. Both important qualities, I thought.

It was after 10 by the time the horses were crammed into the horsebox. A sheep and her crippled lamb were put in the passenger seat, a few dogs stuffed in behind them, and they were driven off to the stable. Eva and I, plus some other helpers, came by car. At midnight we were sitting in Willie's kitchen, ravenously eating good wholesome farmhouse fare of Mother's Pride bread and processed cheese while I wondered if I'd be able to pitch my tent for the first time in the dark. Willie lent me a powerful torch, which helped, and rather to my surprise I got it up easily apart from kneeling in a cowpat. And also to my surprise I felt safe and happy in the night although the field was some way from the house. It was the first time I'd slept alone in a tent.

Next day I was up bright and early, and expecting a clamour of activity by 8.30 in a farming household of five children, I knocked at the door. Silence. I knocked again and Willie appeared in his pyjamas and very kindly cooked me breakfast. I was in Ireland quite a while before it sank in that the Irish don't get up early. Even farmers would emerge from their rooms rubbing their eyes at 9.30, and when I first made the mistake of answering the B&B question "When would you like breakfast?"with "8 o'clock please" I was firmly put in my place. "We'll make it 9 o'clock, shall we?"

Most Saturdays are horse-show days so Willie and his sons were busy getting the show jumpers ready. The ubiquitous Eva was around, however, and helped me saddle the larger of the two grey mares for my eagerly anticipated try-out. I ran what I hoped looked like an expert eye over her and my hand down her legs, trying to remember choice bits of *Buying a Pony* advice from my childhood books. 'The pony should have a nice wide forehead and large kind eyes' – tick that one off – 'a broad chest, sloping shoulders, slanting pasterns and round hooves'. OK for these too. 'Avoid a horse with a neck like a plank of wood'. That one had Kate and me falling about with laughter since Sonnet's neck could have come straight from the timber yard. This pony, however, had a powerful arched neck like a Leonardo da Vinci horse, and with her white coat, dappled grey on the quarters and abundant mane and tail, she fitted her name: Belle. She also had a rather endearing military moustache.

I was pleased to find my saddle and the Peruvian head collar fitted perfectly and that my improvised bit attachment also worked well. I rode nervously out of the yard; it had been at least 10 years since I'd been in charge of a horse and several months since Belle had been ridden. Everyone had advised me that I must buy a fit pony or it would be prone to saddle sores and other health problems. They had also told me to get myself in shape for riding or I would suffer a similar fate. I reckoned Belle and I would just have to get fit together. I was already thinking in terms of 'we' after only about half a mile. Belle was very fresh from her months of inactivity and night in the stable. She walked briskly along, ears sharply pricked, eyes wide, nostrils dilated, ready to shy at any strange object. But when a car came, she passed the most important test of being quiet in traffic. She had smooth, comfortable paces and was responsive to the aids. I also tested her willingness to stand quietly when tied – a very important point – while I went into a shop to get something to eat (I hadn't liked to hang around Willie's at meal times but there were no restaurants nearby so I was getting pretty hungry by 3 o'clock in the afternoon). She was also the right height, given all the mounting and dismounting I was going to do: about 14.2hh.

When I returned to the stable yard I was almost sure that Belle would be my choice, but I still had to try her with saddlebags. She didn't seem to mind when I heaved them onto her back (although they were lighter than usual without the tent etc) and walked along quietly enough when I gingerly led her down the road. I had a hard time swinging my leg over the hump of the bag behind the saddle when I mounted, but Belle stood calmly and again walked willingly under the unaccustomed weight and encumbrance. I was hugely pleased and relieved to find the bags so trouble-free; all I had to do now was finish making the belly strap to prevent them from bouncing up and down when I trotted.

There was still the dark grey pony to try out; Willie had been particularly enthusiastic about this mare and so was I when I first saw her. She was prettier that Belle with more quality, but she was quite a bit smaller and lacked Belle's air of reliability and common sense. She had been nervous and difficult to catch in the corral and when I approached her to put on the bridle she threw up her head and rolled her eyes in fear. At some stage in her life she must have been roughly treated; I didn't want a head-shy animal. My early negative feelings were reinforced during the subsequent ride. The pony was nervous of cars and had a hard mouth. She was actually a very comfortable ride but I just didn't like her so wasn't willing to see any of her good points. I'd decided on Belle and all that was left was to find out whether I could afford her.

In Willie's bathroom, turned face to the wall lest it discourage customers, is a cautionary verse about buying a horse from an Irishman, 'Caveat Emptor'. In this poem there was no difficulty in getting the Irishman to talk about the deal in the first place, yet I spent the rest of Saturday trying to gain an audience with Willie. I sat in the yard sewing my saddle straps and hoping to waylay him during his brief appearances, or lurked in the kitchen where his hospitable wife fed me cups of tea while visitors and family came and went, wondering who I was and what I was doing there. I began to ask the same questions myself; it was a good lesson in humility. In England and Dublin my plans had excited interest and admiration, puffing my ego into a buoyant state. Here at Aille Cross people had other things on their minds; the first trek of the year was imminent with many preparations necessary: all the horses had to be shod, the tack checked and allocated, the hotel reservations confirmed and picnic food bought. No wonder Willie was hard to pin down. In the end I made an appointment for a business talk at 10 o'clock on Sunday. I felt so powerless that I looked on mutely as Belle was loaded into a horsebox with other trek ponies. It was Eva who gently told the boys that I was hoping to buy the pony so would want to go riding on her today.

Willie had suggested that I join his trek so that I could get to know the pony and the local terrain before heading out on my own. It seemed a good idea but I didn't want to commit myself until Belle finally became mine and that happy event receded further when the appointed 10 o'clock came and Willie was banging on horse shoes and obviously couldn't be disturbed. I hung around, clearing my throat and passing the wrong tools until he gave up and came to sit beside me on the bench. My heart pounded as I said that I wanted to buy Belle (he already knew that) and what would be the price. "I've already told you it would be somewhere between 700 and 800 (punts or Irish pounds (IR£))." "Did you?" I couldn't remember having that conversation. "Would you, um, consider 600?" Willie turned to look at me. "I can get more than that in the market," he said, "for horse meat." Of course that concluded the conversation, as he knew it would. "I can't possibly sell for less than 775 with the new set of shoes." I agreed. What else could I do? Translated into sterling his price was about £650, which didn't sound so bad, though it was well over the £500 I'd given myself as a ceiling. But she was a good pony, not just for my purposes but for anyone's, so I should be able to get a good price for her when I sold her.

So on May 6th 1984 I finally became the owner of the pony of my childhood dreams. I rode exultant down the narrow Irish lanes and all those birthday-cake wishes crowded together as I said aloud, "You're mine! You're mine!"

Chapter 5

I couldn't quite believe that I was a horse owner again after 24 years. I kept visiting Belle in her stable to make sure she was real. And I asserted my ownership by changing her name. She was now Mollie, named after the vain pony in *Animal Farm* that hides ribbons in her stall, runs away from the fighting and finally defects from the cause. Since this was 1984, a nod towards George Orwell seemed appropriate and I wondered whether my mare would stick with me through thick or thin. There was a touch of vanity about her: she obviously dyed her mane – why else would the roots be dark?

When I shook hands with Willie over the purchase of Belle/Mollie I also told him I'd like to join the trek for the agreed price of IR£10 since I would now be riding my own pony and would camp rather than stay in hotels with the rest of the group. The trek would begin the following day when the horses, including Mollie, would be transported to Oughterard, the beginning of the Connemara Trail, to be introduced to their riders.

There were five in the group: two couples and a single woman. All were experienced riders, and must have thought I was very strange, going off to sleep in a tent at the end of each day. I was in too much pain to worry about what they thought. My plan had been to get riding-fit gradually by walking on my own feet a good part of each day, so six to eight hours in the saddle was pure torture; I had stabbing pains in my knees and my bottom was so sore I considered a transplant. When we dismounted for a snack I had to stand for a while admiring the view while persuading my legs to straighten so I could walk normally.

On the first day we had a picnic in the grounds of a ruined castle, while the horses grazed the close-cropped grass. A sign said that it was Aughnanure Castle, but there was no other information. These days it is an established tourist attraction owned by Heritage Ireland, with helpful information boards telling you what you are seeing and a ticket booth – and no admission for horses. On our trek I wandered around inside the tower and through the tumbled ruins, making up the history as I went. As we munched our sandwiches Willie gave us a few facts, with embellishments from one of the group who knew his Irish history. The Norman part was extended by the O'Flahertys as a defence against rival clans in the 14th and 15th centuries. Supposedly the old gate into Galway carries an inscription which reads something like 'Oh Lord protect me from the fearsome O'Flahertys'. They were imaginative hosts: under the chair of the guest of honour in the long, splendid dining room there was a trap door, ready to open at the flick of a switch if the guest had not behaved appropriately. I liked the story about the lady pirate, Gráinne O'Malley, who married into the O'Flaherty clan. She was captured by the wicked English and brought before Queen Elizabeth I who, having heard of her exuberant dancing, commanded a performance. Gráinne danced her way out of an open window and escaped.

As the trek progressed I became a little more used to those hours in the saddle and appreciated this chance to get to know Mollie and discover what she could do. And that included dealing with bogs. This being the first trek of the season, Willie had to prepare the trails as we went, cutting branches to provide footing over the squelchy bits. I was amazed that the horses would walk over these and they also walked happily over a long rubber strip that Willie used to cover a particularly tricky stretch. It was a holy carpet, having been used to cushion the wheels of the Popemobile during John-Paul's visit to Ireland. Despite these bridges, two of the horses slipped off the prepared route and sunk up to their bellies in bog. It was terrifying to watch, so I couldn't imagine what it was like for the riders. One woman hopped off onto firm ground as the horse went in but the other stayed put, frozen with fear, and Willie had to tell her what to do. Once free from the weight of the rider, the horses managed to get out – after a struggle. Willie was very calm about it all so I suppose it happens fairly regularly. Thank goodness Mollie understood bogs and walked quietly and carefully over the branches and matting.

Apart from learning how a horse copes with bogs, I discovered that they can swim in the sea. Mannin Bay has a long, sandy beach and we had come prepared with our swimsuits. I was quietly sure that I wasn't going to immerse myself in the Atlantic Ocean in May, but it was a sunny day and no-one dared drop out. With Willie leading the way, we rode into the water until we could feel the horse lose its footing on the seabed and start swimming, with just its eyes and nostrils above the water like a hippo. A strange feeling, but not as cold as I feared because the horse's body keeps you warm. As well as this dip in the sea we frolicked up and down the sand dunes, galloped on the beach and generally had a good time.

The frolicking continued through our farewell dinner when we had a singsong in the bar. The barman was obviously used to Willie's groups and handed out song sheets so we could get the words right. My favourite was about the train that used to run from Ennis to Kilkee in Co Clare. This railway was built around 1860 and wasn't very reliable as the song points out. The Irish then, as now, were sensitive to criticism and the rail company sued the song writer, but when he failed to turn up at court on the appointed day because the train was late the judge dismissed the case.

At breakfast the next morning I learned what I had missed by retiring to my tent. One of the men, still in frolicsome mood, dressed up in a nightie, doused himself in his wife's perfume, and tip-toed into Willie's room to play a seduction scene. When Willie didn't see the joke he sneaked his clothes away and hung them from the chandelier in the hotel's reception area to be discovered by the other guests in the morning. Poor Willie, but I reckon it served him right for teasing me so much over an incident a few nights earlier when a very drunk man tried to find his way into my tent after the bar closed. It was actually rather scary, particularly after his friend said, "I'm not waiting for ye, Willie" and drove off, so the boozy voice outside said I'd have to let him in because he couldn't now get home. He stumbled around outside for a while, tripping over guy ropes and eventually went away, presumably to sleep in a ditch. When I told the group the name of my would-be visitor there was much hilarity.

Only someone with Willie's local knowledge could have devised this trek. He told me about the challenges and obstructions that were put in his way when he first planned it in the 1970s – and he is still leading it 40 years later. Little has changed. The route cuts through the roadless, watery wedge of land that makes up most of Connemara, running up mountains flaming yellow with gorse, through dark forests, and along the disused Galway to Clifden railway line which provided our best canters. Each day had its own highlight and, for me, its lesson in cross-country riding – a lesson I was afraid would be wasted, for how was I to find my way with only half-inch-to-the-mile maps and a compass to guide me? The maps had looked so detailed in the shop, but none of Willie's paths were marked on the Galway sheet. Nevertheless, I learned that Mollie would ford a river with water swirling above her knees, picking her way carefully over slippery stones, deal calmly with bogs, gallop on the beach, swim in the sea, and jump low stone walls.

For the middle few days of the trek the group stayed at Clifden, at the tip of the Connemara peninsula. The misty blue mountains known as the Twelve Bens or the Twelve Pins had been part of the view for a couple of days, but now we were close by them, drenched by sudden rain storms and then drying in the bursts of May sunshine. Last year's dead bracken coated their sides, contrasting with the bare grey rocks of their summits – quartzite, I was told, which had resisted erosion, hence their rugged outline.

Clifden marked a dividing of the ways. After our day on Mannin beach, the group had their final evening in the hotel, and I had my last horseless night in the tent. Mollie was also having her last night with equine company, although she didn't know it. She might have absconded if she had. The next morning I helped Willie round up the horses, saddled and bridled Mollie with her Peruvian head collar and detachable bit, retrieved the saddlebags from the luggage vehicle, and negotiated with the hotel for Mollie to share my tent space in the orchard. The plan was to ride with the group until lunchtime, then head back to Clifden for the night while they continued east.

After warm goodbyes and exchanging of addresses, the group went one way and Mollie and I went the other. I was brimming with mixed feelings: excitement, nervousness, relief, anxiety. This was it. Mollie's feelings were more straightforward. She was appalled. Without the other horses to follow, my lovely keen mare became a sulky plodder, only livening up when she realised we were approaching the field where she'd spent the previous night. When we passed the turn-off her disappointment was crushingly clear, and for the rest of the journey back to the hotel she tried to turn around in the road or shied at manhole covers and plastic bags. It was probably years since she was out without the company of other horses.

If Mollie was despondent, the enormity of what I had set out to do had me quivering with anxiety. I had never tethered Mollie before and had no idea how she would take to it, and my route plans had been kept deliberately vague. All I knew was that my next night would be in Cleggan, Connemara's most westerly town, followed by a loop round Lough Mask so I could visit John Daly, then head south along the coast with no final destination in mind. When I reached the hotel these preoccupations were replaced by a far more pressing problem: I couldn't get into the grounds. Cattle grids blocked both the front and back entrances, and there were no side gates. It was 7 o'clock at night and I couldn't think what to do. I had started rather vaguely leading Mollie back up the road looking for a field or a farmer (but too timid to ask the farmers I saw walking down the road) when I heard a shout. "Hi! How are things?" It was Donna and Peter, two Americans who were staying at the hotel and who had joined us for that day's ride. I explained the problem. "Well, did you ask the hotel manager?"

"Um, no, actually ..." Within minutes Peter and the manager had returned with a couple of planks which they laid over the grid and Mollie walked placidly into the grounds.

The Americans took one look at my tiny tent and cooking stove, and invited me to dinner. "After you've settled Mollie." Time to try out the tether. The corkscrew picket went easily into the ground and felt firm. I attached the padded hobble to Mollie's foreleg, clipping one end of the rope to its ring and tying the other to the picket. Then I stood back and watched. Mollie was too intent on grazing to make a fuss, so I changed my clothes and went in to dinner. It was an interrupted meal. Each time I went out to check on Mollie she was standing pathetically, foreleg stretched out, obviously assuming from her previous experiences of such situations that she'd better stand still until rescued. Each time I had to lead her around to get her used to the idea that she could walk with this gizmo round her leg, and each time she made a major performance of it, lifting her feet very high and giving little snorts of anxiety. She also made a performance of rejecting my nice new collapsible plastic bucket after I'd scrambled down a muddy slope to collect some water for her. Even the hotel's metal bucket was eyed with suspicion.

During that first night of being a horse owner I felt like a new mother just home from hospital with her baby: 'Is she still breathing?' Or in this case 'Is she still munching?' I could hear the steady chomp chomp near the tent, and when it ceased I had to climb reluctantly out of my sleeping bag, put on my boots, and show Mollie once again that being at the end of her tether didn't mean she was incapacitated. She was a slow learner. Each time I found her with her leg stretched out and an accusing expression in her eyes; each time I had to lead her back to the picket while she did her little anxious snorts. Neither of us got much sleep.

I had agreed with Donna and Peter that they would come and see me off at 10 o'clock so I got up at 7 to be sure of being ready in time. I gave Mollie a nosebag full of oats – a parting present from Willie – and prepared my tea and porridge. The sight of all my stuff laid out on the grass filled me with dismay. How had I accumulated so much? The tent, sleeping bag and Thermarest mattress fitted nicely in the centre part along with my (very few) clothes, but then there was my little radio, a couple of books, maps, my stove and some food, and various odds and ends. When it was all in and zipped up I could barely lift the bag from the ground, let alone heave it over Mollie's back. "This isn't going to work!" I muttered, but of course it did, because it had to, and Mollie was very patient with all the uncomfortable banging and thumping.

I was pleased to have a send-off; as a lone traveller I missed being able to say something like "Here we go!" to a companion, yet something is needed when heading out on an expedition. More practically, I was grateful to have someone hold Mollie while I mounted; getting my leg over all that luggage wasn't easy. A few minutes after waving goodbye I had to dismount again, having forgotten the cattle grid. The planks were still there and once again Mollie walked over without fuss and I rode west through Clifden, taking the steep hill bordered by moorland, signposted 'Cleggan'.

Chapter 6

Nicky had been recommended to me as a possible source of a Connemara pony. When I had phoned her from Galway she explained that she had no ponies for sale, but the friendly welcome in her voice when she suggested that I might like to camp at their place in Cleggan shaped my plans. Cleggan is only a half-day ride from Clifden, so a logical stop for my first night. Besides, how could I resist staying at a farm with a single-digit phone number?

Riding out of Clifden I felt as though I was sitting on an armchair. The soft middle section of the saddlebag partly covered the cantle and made a nice back support if I adopted my favourite sack-of-potatoes posture. It reminded me of a dream I'd had while planning the trip. I was all saddled up and ready to go when the horse turned round and said sharply "Don't you think you can do better that that?" I saw its point; instead of a saddle there was a blue kitchen chair on its back.

People stared at my strange luggage or used the 'don't stare, dear' technique – a quick glance, look away as though there's nothing abnormal, then stop in their tracks to gaze at my departing figure. At least Mollie disregarded all those strange lumps attached to her saddle, not to mention the one in the saddle, and walked on cheerfully enough.

I took a minor road along a deep inlet – a fjord really – called Streamstown Bay. It was a sunny day with clear views across the blue water to the craggy green peninsula beyond. Mollie was in a reflective mood, probably wondering what she'd done to deserve such punishment. Every so often she'd wake out of her reverie to shy at rocks, drains or white lines painted on the road, and that woke me out of my own reveries. It was a side of her I hadn't seen when riding in company; then she was the essence of common sense, ignoring all the imaginary hazards that sent other ponies scuttling across the road.

This was rocky, gale-swept Connemara; a few hunch-backed trees leant away from the prevailing wind, but on this still, sunny May morning the little fields by the road were full of sheep or flowers; there were bluebells, plantains and cow parsley in some, a white blanket of daisies in others, and great bunches of king cups and marsh marigolds in rushy water meadows. The road ran between steep banks covered with primroses and violets. I didn't mind Mollie's slow pace.

"You really must go to Omey Island," Nicky had said. "You can have a wonderful gallop on the beach at low tide." And indeed, we arrived at a half-mile expanse of rippled yellow sand fronted by sea-weedy boulders being picked over by two oyster catchers. Mollie seemed to have forgotten all her seaside experiences and made a terrific fuss about stepping onto the sand and rocks, although completely unfazed by a hysterically barking sheepdog. I was tempted to take the saddlebags off and have a really good gallop, but the memory of the effort needed to heave the pack back into position, stopped me. I contented myself with cantering in the direction of the island, with the dog in hot pursuit, before making a large circle and galloping back.

I arrived at Cleggan in the afternoon; an attractive village of a few shops lining the waterfront, with the farm, backed by mountains dotted with white sheep, clearly visible across the bay. The family were out, but Nicky's mother-in-law showed me a large field for Mollie and the back lawn for my tent.

To my relief there was no sign of any saddle sore or rubbed place under the bags so obviously the sheepskin and towel were doing their stuff. Mollie was thrilled at being turned loose after her tethered night, and walked off with that funny bent-leg walk that horses adopt when planning to have a roll. I watched her kicking her feet in the air and grunting with pleasure, before leaving to put up my tent. There were still hours of daylight left so I went off to explore the neighbourhood and in particular to look for a 'megalithic tomb' marked on the map. These dolmen tombs are fairly common in this part of Ireland and are some of the island's earliest archaeological remains, dating from around 3000BC. The purpose of the structure – side stones supporting a huge capstone – is not clear, but I wondered how on earth the builders managed to lever the giant stones into position. Probably there were more large trees around in those days.

When I got back to the house the family had returned and I was immediately enveloped into the easy atmosphere of farm life. Nicky's husband, Hugh, inherited the farm in a semi-derelict state and was gradually restoring it to productivity; a race against time as he was losing his sight. A peat fire burned in the grate and blocks of peat were stacked up on each side of the huge fireplace. "I don't suppose you ever have to buy coal?" I asked. "Well, not yet, but turf is still a fossil fuel, you know. And they've already used it all up in the Aran Islands, so it won't last forever." The phone rang. "OK," said Hugh, "I'll be right there."

One of the neighbour's cows was stuck in a ditch. By the time we got there the cow had been hauled out but the calf, which she had tried to reach when it fell in a drainage ditch, had drowned. The poor cow walked miserably along, bellowing for her lost child, but the farmer was quietly relieved to have saved her. "A few more hours and she'd have been dead," he said. "Cows don't last long in water." I was fascinated by his singsong accent, so different from the flatter tones of Galway. He went on to discuss what animal was killing the newborn lambs. "I wouldn't wonder if it wasn't a pine marten," he said but he pronounced it "paine mairrten".

Crawling into my tent around midnight, glowing from hospitality for the second consecutive evening, I reflected that it was a good thing I was going to start trekking properly tomorrow or I would get soft. My destination was a youth hostel at Killary, about 20 miles away, at the tip of a peninsula. Yesterday I'd been told by a cyclist that it was one of the prettiest hostels in Ireland; there was no phone so I couldn't check whether grazing was available.

Mollie had also enjoyed the hospitality and had no intention of leaving her spacious field the next morning. Most horse owners are familiar with the rage and despair that accompanies the trudge around a large field of long, dew-soaked grass in pursuit of their animal. Mollie kept on with her eating, an ear cocked for my soothing pleasantries and a sneer on her lips, until I was 10 feet or so away, then took off at a brisk trot. I'd left her head collar on, just in case, but she understood the just in case perfectly well and made sure I was never within grabbing distance.

"Come on Mollie, good girl!" I said in gentle horse-loving tones as I walked towards her with equicide in my heart. After half an hour I realised she was not going to get bored with this little game and I'd have to resort to bribery. The family was out, but fortunately I had spotted a sack of horse nuts outside the kitchen door. I'd discovered during the trek that Mollie didn't know what to do with a titbit, having tried her with apples, carrots, barley sugar, Polo mints and sugar lumps, all thoughtfully purchased from shops along the way. She'd inspect each one, smelling it carefully with a look of astonishment on her face, then throw her head up with a 'you can't fool me' gesture and refuse to have anything more to do with it. She liked recognisable food in a recognisable container and no messing about.

Filling a bucket with horse nuts I went back to the field and got exactly the same reaction. Mollie let me get a little closer and showed interest in the bucket's contents, but however stealthily I reached out my hand she always saw it coming and trotted off. However, my arrival with a bucket hadn't gone unnoticed by the herd of bullocks in the neighbouring field and they galloped up and down the fence bellowing encouragement whenever I seemed to be approaching them. Eventually Mollie's greed got the better of her and I managed to take hold of her head collar. Typically, once caught she accepted the situation with equanimity and I was able to clip on the lead rein and start for the gate. Here I was confronted with a new problem: Mollie's gate led into the bullocks' field where another gate, at right angles to the first, opened onto the road. Both were secured by the same piece of rope so either both were closed or both open. The bullocks were clustered excitedly by the gates, waiting for me to deliver the goodies in the bucket. I had to tie Mollie to the gate-post and leave her eating her horse-nuts while I unfastened the rope securing the two gates. Then I propped both gates shut and started to climb back over the stone wall into Mollie's field. The top boulders gave way. I fell heavily with a squawk of pain, Mollie took fright, pulled back and broke her lead rein, the gate swung open and three bullocks escaped into the road. I was near to tears. My attempts to drive the bullocks back into the field only resulted in the escape of two more; I had a bruised arm, a gashed ankle, Mollie was once again enjoying her freedom and I'd committed the cardinal sin of damaging a fence and letting out livestock. The wall was easily rebuilt but I could see that I'd never drive the bullocks back without someone else stopping the rest of the herd oozing through the open gates. I returned to the house and was fortunate to find that a friend of Hugh's had just arrived. Together we succeeded in driving the animals back in their field.

Mollie was even less willing to be bribed a second time. It was two hours since I'd first gone out to the field and rain was now falling steadily. I cursed horses and Ireland and childhood dreams until Mollie suddenly got bored with the whole business and allowed me to take her head collar and lead her (successfully this time) through the gates to the house, while I told her what I thought of her and reminded her of the price of horse meat.

It was raining hard as I rode out of Cleggan. "A grand soft morning!" exclaimed an old farmer as I plodded past, scowling, with the rain dripping down my neck. I'd meant to buy lunch provisions in Cleggan but was in too bad a mood to make the diversion to the shops so trusted to luck that I'd find a grocer along the way. Which I did, though the notice outside the general store-cum-post office said 'Closed for Lunch 1–2'. It was 1.50. I tied Mollie with a long rope so she could graze (not that she deserved it), hunched myself in my leaking anorak (promoted as a major breakthrough in rain gear) and settled down to wait. At 2.15 someone ambled along and opened the shop; I bought a yoghurt and apple and ate them in a growing pool of water near the door. I also had a parcel of unwanted maps and other odds and ends to send off – I had to lighten my saddlebags. While the post mistress was helpfully looking for brown paper and string, a small child came running in excitedly with the news that there was a white horse outside. Everyone went out to look while I tied up my parcel and then went outside to retrieve the post mistress so she could weigh it and take my money. I emerged just in time to release Mollie from a tangle of rope round her legs; she was starting to panic and use brute force. At least I'd had the sense to tie her with a slip knot.

I rode around Ballynakill harbour in improving weather and better spirits. "Lovely day!" called out a farmer as he approached. "That's a grand way of seeing the country." We chatted about my plans and he admired

Mollie and asked how much I'd paid for her. Then he looked at her teeth to check her age. Irish countrymen find it almost impossible to admire a horse without looking in its mouth. Our meetings took on a set form: "Beautiful day, lovely mare! What did you pay for her?" followed by speculation on her age. By the end I expected Mollie to open her mouth automatically when anyone approached. I gave up saying she was nine. No-one agreed with me; estimates varied between five and 15. And I gave up giving the true purchase price since I got tired of suggestions that I'd been done.

When we turned northward away from the sea the scenery became austere. Peat bogs stretched away towards low hills dramatically backed by grey clouds. Mollie was stodging along and we needed some variety so I took a turf cutters' track across the moor, hoping it would link up with the road the other side. It was even bleaker in the middle of the moor; green-brown bogland with a rain-filled sky overhead. The only splashes of colour were provided by the wrecks of cars discarded along the way and those belonging to a group of turf-cutters who stopped their work and watched me in astonishment. I asked them if the track joined the one to Tully Cross. "Sure it does, but you'd do better to go back." Once I persuaded them that I wanted to be away from the road they gave me directions.

Turf cutting seemed to be a family affair. Men and women worked at it together and their children played around the wrecked cars or sat around with their parents in chilly groups drinking tea from thermos flasks. I learned all about turf during a pub conversation a few days later. I still had difficulty remembering to call it turf; peat is what they call it in other parts of the world. Someone told me about the visitor who asked "Are you going to get peat?" and got the reply, "No, Pete's got the flu, I'm going for George." My informant told me that peat is only used in gardens; turf is cut from a peat bog. Most rural houses are sold along with their turbary rights or sections of bog. Householders can either cut the turf themselves or pay someone to do it. First, the top six inches of heather, grass and other vegetation has to be removed before the potential fuel is reached. Although machines are used now, in the 1980s many people still cut turf by hand, using a slane or spade with a wing which cuts neat bars of the chocolaty peat (the dictionary definition is 'decomposed vegetable matter partly carbonised'). A bar of turf is about 14 inches long, with the best quality found near the surface, one to three bars down, although it's still good to 10 bars but this is poor fuel. The bars are left to dry for a week then stacked into neat pyramids of eight, and left for a further two weeks to dry out completely. Horses and drays (a type of toboggan) or donkeys with panniers were still used in some parts of the country to collect the turf. Turbary was worth about IR£1,000 an acre. My pub friend estimated this would yield 12,000 trailer loads of turf at a total cost of 5p per year.

The threatening rain kept off and with the help of my compass I joined my intended road just as the sun broke through. Climbing a heathery hillock, I came upon such a beautiful view of sea and islands, I decided to give Mollie a rest from the saddlebags and ease my aching body. Despite my six days in the saddle with Willie I still felt stiff and sore after a few hours of riding, and needed a break from time to time. Mollie's bridle arrangement worked well; I could quickly undo the side straps and remove the bit so she could graze more comfortably. It was rather nice of me, I thought, to ease Mollie's back at the expense of my own. Although the mailing of that map parcel had rid the saddlebags of some of their weight, it still took a huge effort to lift them into place. Out of view of passing cars and their curious drivers, I could relax completely, propped up against a sun-warmed rock. I shut my eyes. . . Waking with a start I saw Mollie's receding figure as she walked briskly back towards Cleggan, but I'd left a trailing rope so it was easy to retrieve her and give her a lecture on gratitude before saddling and bagging up again.

Killary was still a good seven miles away and it was now late afternoon. I kicked Mollie into a trot (she was becoming very idle) and made good progress along the little-used lane that ran past lumpy green headlands of short-cropped grass, shingle beaches and a dark blue sea. It was all incredibly beautiful in the evening light. Just as I was wondering where I'd find provisions for supper I passed another of those handy post-offices-cum-shops found in remote areas of Ireland. "Jesse James rides again!" said the boy with a giggle as I paid for my bread, milk, eggs and sausages.

I led Mollie the last few miles to the youth hostel. We both needed a rest from the saddle. The road dropped steeply down to Killary Bay through tall trees and past a manor house just visible up a long drive, bright with rhododendrons. There were lush green fields on my left and heathery hills on my right, cropped almost bare by sheep. A farmer stopped to talk and I told him that I was looking for grazing. "You won't find any around here."

"But what about those fields there?"

"Oh no, an English lady owns those. You won't get permission, definitely not."

The youth hostel is a converted coast-guard station picturesquely set by a small harbour full of fishing boats. I tied Mollie to a railing and went to look for the warden. He was surprised and a little depressed by my mode of transport and confirmed that I wouldn't get permission to put Mollie in one of the lush fields; they were green because the grass was being grown for hay.

"I'd let you put her in the garden," he said "but I'm trying to grow the hedge. I've been trying for three years." I looked at the garden; it was tiny – about 15 by 30 feet – with a few blades of grass struggling through the hard ground and a washing line at the far end hung with jeans and damp socks. It had one asset: it was completely enclosed by a wire mesh fence against which a few leafless twigs were attempting to become a hedge. The warden agreed that Mollie and the hedge could probably coexist and suggested I talk to the fishermen who were mending their nets on the jetty. Most had small farms nearby and should be able to let me have some hay. I went out and found Mollie standing in a huge pool of urine with some giggling hostellers hovering near the shallows. I disclaimed any association with her and approached the fishermen who glanced up briefly with bored 'Here come the silly questions' expressions. They became more interested when I explained my problem. "There's not even enough grass this year for the sheep," one said. "We've had no rain since Easter." That morning's downpour in Cleggan hadn't reached Killary, apparently. A fisher-farmer agreed to sell me some hay, and while he went to collect it in his van I settled Mollie in her night's accommodation. Getting in was tricky; there was a small gate leading off the rocky beach and then the washing line to duck under, but she followed me willingly enough in the expectation of peace and plenty. Explaining about the imminent arrival of best Connemara hay, I left her crossly ripping up blades of grass while I went to fetch water. I knew she was thirsty but the wretched animal once again refused to drink out of a bucket; it wasn't even plastic, it belonged to the hostel. It appeared that she'd led such a natural organic life that she could only drink from streams.

The farmer returned with hay, which cost me IR£1, and Mollie refused to eat it. As for me, it was past 9 o'clock and I was hungry. While I cooked and ate my eggs and bacon, I chatted with the other hostellers from Switzerland, Germany and the USA. Every now and then, out of the corner of my eye, I'd see a white form pass in front of the window. Mollie was pacing up and down and I was sure she was looking for water so went out with a Swiss girl to have another go at persuading her to drink. When I approached her she gave me a scornful look and turned away, but the Swiss girl talked to her in German, dabbled fingers in the water, and lifted the bucket to the pony's nose. 'Oh, water!' said Mollie's expression and she had a drink.

Next morning I found Mollie standing sulkily by the untouched and expensive pile of hay, but when I tied her up to prepare her for the day's work she realised it was her last chance to eat for a while, and started tucking in. I decided to go for a walk and leave her munching.

The cyclist who'd told me that Killary was the prettiest hostel in Ireland had good taste. It lies on a narrow peninsula south of the nine-mile-long fjord, Killary Harbour. Across this narrow strip of water, the Mweelrea Mountains, which include a 2,600-foot peak, rise abruptly from the rocky shore. It was a brilliantly clear and sunny morning and from my viewpoint near the tip of the peninsula I could see the islands of Inishturk and Inishbofin in one direction and a skyline of mountain silhouettes in the other. Red and blue fishing boats rested in the harbour below the hostel where, picked out by the sun, I could see my white horse. I felt almost euphorically happy and adventurous and looked longingly at a grassy track running close to the sea's edge. To get onto it with Mollie I would have to dismantle a stone wall and I didn't want to risk riding several miles only to meet an impassable obstruction. I now know (2011) that this track follows the shore for about five miles down the southern bank of the Killary fjord; it would have been a lovely ride. The hostel is closed for renovations and Mollie's tiny field is now carpeted with long grass. There is no sign of a hedge. On the wall a new plaque proudly commemorates Ludwig Wittgenstein's stay there in 1948. This gloomy Austrian philosopher lived alone in the cottage for four months: thinking, writing, tearing up his notes, and learning the names of English seabirds.

Mollie refused to leave the garden. Not because of the remaining hay and five blades of grass, but she jibbed at the idea of ducking under the washing line and then squeezing through the narrow gate. In the end I had to take down the line. I wondered if we'd ever make a smooth start in the morning; despite rising at 7 it was 10.30 before we left, taking the road inland rather than risking the coastal path. The weather was still cool and sunny and my euphoric mood soon returned with the views across fields of bluebells to craggy, seamed mountains. After an hour the first car passed and screeched to a halt in front of me. A man jumped out and announced that he was Tom from Gowlaun and that he'd seen me yesterday. What a grand way of seeing the country and how much had I paid for the pony? Hmm... about seven years old, he'd say...

I like lakes with names like Lough Muck, particularly when their unpolluted waters are fringed with bluebells and yellow gorse. The small lake dwindled into a river then expanded into the long sausage of Lough Fee. Time for a leg stretch. I considerately loosened the girths and walked along the side of the road with the lead rope loose in my hand, singing 'Molly Malone'. "Cockles and muss-els, alive, alive..." Mollie stopped dead. "Come on you stupid old cow," I said, hauling on her rope. No response. Looking back I saw that the saddle and saddlebags had slipped and now hung below her belly.

Oh heck, would I be able to undo the many buckles before she realised the unpleasantness of her situation and took off? But Mollie didn't look panicked, she looked resigned, and stood still while I fumbled with the straps. Once the saddle and bags lay in the road she started to graze. I patted her and told her she was quite sensible after all, and that I was fairly stupid not to consider the effects of a rolling walk and gravity on unevenly weighted saddlebags. I was glad this wasn't a busier road as I went through the saddling order of sheepskin, towel (put under saddlebags to absorb sweat), saddle, do up girth loosely, saddlebags, seven straps fastenings, then final girth tightening. Except that I forgot the latter so after five minutes or so the whole thing happened again. This time Mollie gave the sort of sigh that my parents gave when I phoned to say I'd missed the train. But she stood still.

Actually it was her fault, since I couldn't tighten the girth when I first put on the saddle because she always blew herself up like a white balloon when she felt me pulling at the straps. I don't know how horses do this – whether it's by taking a deep breath or tensing their stomach muscles – but it causes a dramatic increase in waist measurement and, in Mollie's case, a fearsome storm in her digestive tract. "Rumble thy bellyful!" I quoted, with my head under the saddle flaps. I gave her earfuls of Shakespeare, Yeats and other poets as she plodded along. One ear would flick back – appreciatively, I thought.

I mounted again and we continued through a great baaing of sheep. A lamb had escaped through the fence and was standing on the far hillside bleating for its mother. Mum was standing her ground, some way inside the fence, calling back. They seemed to have reached a stalemate. "No, you come to *me*." I thought that I should do something but didn't know what, so left them to their own devices.

Approaching the pretty village of Leenaun I was intrigued to see a sign 'Shellfish training programme' and wondered what they were being trained to do. Leenaun was set a-buzzing by my arrival, especially when I tied up outside a shop to buy a snack. This was the gateway to 'Joyce's Country' which I'd always thought referred to James Joyce but has no literary associations; it got its name from an ordinary landowner. Heading south, the very lovely road follows a deep river valley between two mountain ranges and is on the tourist itinerary. I was passed by several coaches with most of the occupants asleep. Joyce's river flows through green fertile fields with prosperous-looking farms tucked into the lower folds of the mountains. One appeared to have a long purple-blue wall edging a copse; my binoculars revealed a field crammed solid with bluebells.

The beautiful views and open countryside made me ambitious and I decided on a short cut over the mountains. If I rode due east, I reckoned that I should intercept my intended road on the other side. At first Mollie was thrilled to feel grass beneath her hooves but then she realised she was going uphill and this was hard work. I got off to prove to her that at least one of us had the willpower to keep climbing despite shortness of breath. I'd planned to cut diagonally across the hillside but was stopped by a fence which apparently ran from the summit to the road. Mollie had been reasonably willing to traverse the hill, but she saw no sense at all in following a fence up a 1,400-foot mountain when there was a perfectly good road running round the base. She made such a fuss I was afraid she'd have a heart attack, so gave in to her demands that we abandon the idea or at least stop for a snack. We did both and the view across to the bluebell field and mountains beyond made our efforts seem worthwhile. For me anyway.

After another hour we came to such a perfect campsite I decided to stop for the night. I'd turned off the tourist route onto a minor road running between a cleft in the mountains. Close by the road a noisy shallow river ran through pasture which gave way to the dead bracken and heather of the hillside. There were plenty of dry flat places for my tent and good grazing for Mollie who was hungry after her deprived night. The ground was firm enough to hold the corkscrew picket, and Mollie could drink from her favourite source of water: a river. There were no houses nearby so I didn't feel too guilty camping without permission.

Eating my soup beside the tent, warm in the evening sun, with my white pony grazing against a backdrop of river and mountains, I was aware of the rightness of the scene. This is what I had imagined my journey would be like, not a horse in a garden under a washing line.

Chapter 7

Mollie clearly believed in leprechauns. We could be slopping along, happily lost in our own thoughts, when suddenly her head would go up, her ears prick so they almost met in the middle and she'd snort and jump at every sound or movement. She'd keep it up for a mile or so, then get bored and slump back into an even plod. By the evening I swear that if she could have found a way of crawling on hands and knees she would, and even when I got off and led her, I had to haul her along like a toy tractor.

Providing her with sufficient water continued to be a challenge. She was quite maddening: except when desperate she'd only drink from natural water sources. Helpful housewives would come running out of their homes in slippers, slopping full buckets of water, and she'd just turn her head away. I was trying to persuade her to approach a lovely rustic water trough and urging her on with uncouth language when I heard "You can lead a horse to water but you can't make it drink!" coming from a tiny bent old man who'd been posing as a hawthorn tree in the shadows. That proverb should be 'You can lead a horse to water but you can't make it think'.

Mollie specialised in making me feel humble and guilty. She was still difficult to catch although I left a long rope trailing so I wouldn't have a repeat of that first morning, and I would be lying if I said there had been much bonding. Sometimes she would stare at me with an air of surprise, as if to say "Goodness, are you still here?" And she sighed a lot. Or she'd look at me, shut her eyes and look away. This is bad enough in people and just not acceptable in a Companion Animal.

That night in Joyce's Country was only the second time I'd used her hobble tether so I was doing my new-mother act of sleeping fitfully, listening out for her cries of distress. Not that you could call Mollie's 'This is the absolute limit!' snort, a cry. It was a noisy expiration of breath through half-closed nostrils, and she did it when she had reached the end of her tether, literally or metaphorically. But at least she'd come to terms with the hobble, although she still walked with an exaggerated high step when it was attached to her leg. The corkscrew was bent in the morning, but still firmly in the ground and I was pleased to have worked out that this is the best way of tethering a pony.

The early morning was clear, but by the time I was ready to leave I could see patches of rain sweeping over the mountains across the valley. It never reached me and I remained dry as I followed the route I'd selected the previous night on the map. There had been a choice of two roads, but how could I resist the one running by rivers called Fooey and Finney? My next night would be spent at Lough Mask House, on the eastern shores of that lake, with John Daly, an expert in all things horsey. He bred Connemaras, rode show jumpers, trained race horses, and owned the house which his cousin, my friend Dorothy, told me was once the home of 'the infamous Captain Boycott'.

The narrow road ran between two mountain ranges where sheep with curly horns grazed the golden-beige tussock grass, then dropped down to Lough Nafooey. Now I was inland it felt warmer. Cuckoos were calling, larks trilling and a pair of dippers bobbed in courtship on the half-submerged boulders of the lake. All morning I'd been looking out for a phone box so I could ring John to warn him of my arrival, and now I saw a shop displaying one of the little green 'Post' signs that indicate a public phone as well as a post office. An old man with a pale cadaverous face and shining blue eyes stood behind the counter. Above him was a hand-lettered sign 'Let nothing disturb you – all things are passing'. I bought my lunch-time snack, which those days mostly consisted of chocolate. And why not? I seldom ate a proper meal. One day I devoured an entire packet of Jaffa Cakes for lunch, and nothing else, but at other times I'd be a paragon of virtue eating brown bread and marmite, fruit and yoghurt. I munched my Crunchie while the postmaster slowly and carefully added up the bill on a scrap of paper. I told him I wanted to make a phone call and wrote down the number. He pointed to a phone box near the shop door where I waited for him to connect me.

John's wife Pat answered the phone. Yes, they were expecting me sometime and this evening would be fine. I told her I should arrive around 7 o'clock. When I paid for the call I asked the postmaster if he had to work long hours. "Oh yes," he said, with his serene smile "if someone's sick you're going to help them out." This tiny post office seemed to be the local telephone exchange and was clearly the hub of this area where many people had no phone. As I was leaving, a customer entered and greeted me like an old friend. "I saw you last night camping. Weren't you afraid?" I could truthfully say no. I was proud of that.

∩ ∩ ∩

On my return visit I found what I hoped was the right post office, but I wasn't sure. Above the door was a bold sign 'Duffy's Finny'. A delicious smell of fried onions greeted me, and a young woman emerged from the kitchen. "Children's lunch." she explained. "Thought I'd better make a stew while things are quiet." I told her about my 1984 visit. "Was this once a telephone exchange?"

"No, that's over the hill that way." I felt a stab of disappointment.

"What I remember most," I said, "is the almost radiant face of the old man who ran it. And there was a sign, something like 'Let nothing trouble you, all things pass'. The woman pointed – and there was the sign, just as I remembered it, handwritten in magic marker on a piece of cardboard cut from a box. "Paddy was my dad!" said Margaret. "He died the year you were here, in 1984. He was 74. I was one of nine children, and he was in his fifties when he had me so he always seemed old. I remember, he got one of us to make that sign. Not everyone liked it – some would say that it wasn't true. But, yes, he was always there if people needed help." We beamed at each other, each with our own memory of him.

∩ ∩ ∩

The mountains were now at my back and the road to Lough Mask was flat and dull. I felt bored and cold; Mollie was bored and sluggish. She couldn't even stir up the energy to look for leprechauns. I had a brief frisson of excitement when we crossed into Co Mayo and another when we crossed back into Co Galway on a bridge over a narrow part of Lough Mask. Now I could see the main lake; it's huge (over nine miles long) and full of little islands, some sporting shrubs or trees like fancy hats.

I'd scribbled down John's directions and eventually we reached a formidable set of stone pillars by a little white gate lodge. Bypassing the cattle grid through a side gate I rode down about a mile of curving drive between fields with cattle-pruned chestnut trees in flower and splendid groups of beeches protected by mossy stone walls. What a contrast with Connemara which has few trees. A grey pony came galloping up and I was terrified that it would be a stallion and want to have his wicked way with Mollie. I waved my whip and it kept its distance, rather to Mollie's disappointment. When I reached the house there was another cattle grid and I couldn't find a gate so I tied Mollie to a tree and went to announce my arrival.

John and Pat and two bouncing Jack Russell terriers greeted me as though I was an old friend. John is taller than I imagined an ex-jockey to be, with all-knowing grey eyes. Pat wouldn't hear of me sleeping in my tent: "I've already made up a bed for you."

"And the mare can spend the night in the orchard," added John. Being such an expert on Connemara ponies I was dying to hear what he thought of her. "Well," he said. "Pat told me she'd passed you on the road about half an hour ago and that you had an absolutely beautiful pony." I smiled smugly. "But she's not, you know. Her head's too big and her back's too long. But the thing is, with that fancy bridle and all the saddle bags those faults don't show." I felt a bit crestfallen but I can't pretend I hadn't noticed Mollie's big head; I thought it might contain a large brain. I turned her loose in the orchard and John and I leaned over the fence and watched her as she had a vigorous roll. "She's not really tired, you know. And she can easily carry the weight." I think he thought I was a bit soft on her. He also told me that the spring grass has as much nutrient in it as oats and that Mollie didn't need any extra food (she'd been telling me she was faint with hunger and close to collapse).

I ate an enormous supper while the family sat around and watched in awe. Of the two children only Alan, a very polite red-headed teenager, was at home. He was a keen and successful show-jumper and showed me the beautiful Connemara stallion he rode in competitions. I asked John whether a stallion wasn't a problem in the show ring. "No, he knows when he's at a show and just concentrates on the work in hand."

While I was eating, John told me stories of his life with horses. Like Willie Leahy, he started horse-dealing at an early age. "My first pony cost IR£2 10s. When I was 15 he won the championship at the Galway show. We sold him for IR£225." Since then John has been involved in every possible horse activity. He's been a jockey and a top-class show jumper (when I heard that he'd competed against Pat Smythe I nearly stopped eating in admiration), has bred and trained race horses and jumpers and a film has been made of his technique of breaking wild Connemara ponies. He can make an animal that has never been touched by a human quiet under the saddle and bit in a couple of hours. He just oozed horse magic.

For as long as the Dalys have lived in Lough Mask House, they have been making money with horses. "When my grandfather was 21, about 1887 that would be, he walked the horses all the way to Dublin and then took them over to England. About 15 or 20, there were. He used drovers' trails – I think he went across the Welsh mountains. He used to stay in tollhouses, turn the horses loose, then round them up the next morning. He took them all the way to Barnet Fair where he got three sovereigns for each horse. He told my father he was terrified going home with all that money in his pocket in case he was robbed."

I asked John about Captain Boycott and why he was infamous. "It's where the word boycott comes from," he said. "He had a tough time of it; he was only doing his job, you know." I didn't know but decided to research it later. It's an interesting story, and provides a little nugget of history highlighting the strained relationship between the indigenous Irish population and the English colonisers.

Captain Boycott had a lease on Lough Mask House and 300 acres of land, and was also employed by Lord Erne – an absentee landlord – to collect the rent owed by the tenant farmers of the area. This was no mean task – the land encompassed over 1,500 acres worked by 38 families. This was in the early days of the Irish Land League, founded by Michael Davitt, with Charles Stewart Parnell as its president (he went on to campaign for Home Rule). The aim of the League was to transfer ownership of the land to the families who worked it – a precursor to the 20th-century political struggles in Africa and South America.

Harvests had failed for several years at a stretch due to bad weather and many tenant farmers were unable or unwilling to pay their rent. Captain

Boycott was reportedly unpopular because of his inflexibility and adherence to petty rules (although John says that he was well liked. "Otherwise he would have been shot.") When, in September 1880, he served eviction notices on 11 families, the area was ripe for rebellion. As the process server, accompanied by local constables, started the eviction process, a booing crowd gathered and pelted the officials with mud and manure, driving them to take refuge in Lough Mask House. Parnell had suggested that local people 'shun' greedy landlords and his advice was taken up by the local priest. Boycott's servants and farm hands were persuaded to leave, shop keepers refused to serve him, and even the little post boy was intimidated. To make matters worse, it was the grain harvest time, and the Boycott household, including the women, had to roll up their sleeves and get the harvest in. But the root vegetables, including turnips and potatoes, remained in the ground, so Captain Boycott wrote a letter to *The Times* explaining his predicament, and describing, in colourful language, the 'howling mob' and the damage they were doing to his land.

This produced a flurry of sympathy from the English and Protestant Irish readers who were already uneasy about the rebellious Irish Catholics, and money was raised for the Boycott Relief Fund to hire a band of Ulster volunteers to bring in the remaining harvest. The press was thrilled at this turn of events, especially in America, and reporters started to gather at Lough Mask. Meanwhile some 50 Ulstermen marched the 14 miles from the train station in Claremorris (no transport, of course, was made available to take them to the house) in pouring rain and settled in tents, haylofts or wherever they could find shelter. Boycott could have coped with a workforce of 50, but his heart must have sunk at the arrival of hundreds of army chaps to protect the volunteers, not to mention the press reporters from England and America, who between them reduced the garden to a quagmire.

In some ways both sides won. The harvest was safely gathered in ('one shilling for every turnip' as Parnell remarked bitterly) and Captain Boycott and his family left Lough Mask House, accompanied by his dog, a parrot in a cage, and little else. He would no doubt have preferred his name to live on in another context. "You see, the farm labourers were Irish-speaking and couldn't say 'ostracise' so they said boycott. And the word stuck," said John. "He was a good horseman, you know. My great grandfather bought this house in 1886."

∩ ∩ ∩

It was lovely to sleep in a real bed without worrying about Mollie. All John's talk of horse-breaking brought on a dream about a group of cowboys dressed in black leather mounted on carousel horses and practising neck-reining and lassoing as they went round and round. In the morning John said that Mollie had succeeded in getting rid of her head collar and I was filled with gloom at the thought of trying to catch her in this horse haven and of finding a black head collar among so many fallen black branches. But John and Pat told me not to worry, to eat my bacon and eggs and they'd find it.

By the time I'd finished packing up, Mollie was standing by the front door dressed in her head collar, and John had cast his expert eye over her and seen something that had escaped me in the daily search for sores: she was scraping her upper hoof with the opposite shoe and had worn away all the hair on her coronet. "You need to see Paddy McDonagh in Shrule. He's the best blacksmith in Ireland." John smiled. "He's a great character. Won all those awards but he's no airs and graces. Rides about on his bicycle. I went to see him once and had a pain in my chest so I mentioned it to Paddy. 'Oh I knew a man who had that,' he said 'it's called angina. But he lived another three weeks, you know.'"

Next door to the house there's a ruined 14th-century castle. Apparently when they built the house in the 1800s they were wondering whether to restore the castle instead but decided against it. Thank goodness. It's a beautiful ruin all covered in ivy and crows, with a grand view of Lough Mask from the top of the battlements. Alan showed me around it and I thought how nerve-wracking it must have been for Pat knowing that whatever she said the children would play there, with sheer drops of 100 feet or so and some very narrow walkways.

When we were chatting over dinner, I'd asked John about scenic rides in the area. I couldn't believe that there were no bridle paths or similar. "Why don't you go to Cong and ride in the grounds of Ashford Castle? Ronald Reagan's going to stay there in a few days' time. They'll be too busy to bother about you."

Cong is a pretty village with a row of pastel-coloured houses, a ruined abbey and tourists. One stopped me and said, "See here, I can't find the entrance to this hotel." I suppose he thought I was just part of the village life. Huge machines were digging a deep hole near the castle gates; presumably a fallout shelter for the American president. Mollie didn't like the machines at all but allowed herself to be led past by one of the workmen. It seemed almost a foolish act of bravery to go in through that arched entrance in the imposing turreted gate lodge. The grounds were full of un-Irish-looking men with short hair and coats and ties, pointing strange devices at the rose bushes. No one asked me what I was doing. I just said "Mornin'!" in an upper-class sort of way and rode up to the castle, which is huge, grey and menacing, along the golf course and through the forest. I was so rigid with nerves I felt like a chunk of wood nailed to the saddle with a grinning mask for a face; my bowels turned to water so I had to get off, tie Mollie up, and go into the woods to dig a little hole. I imagined there was a secret serviceman behind every tree and they'd all rush forward after I'd finished to see what sort of explosive device I'd buried.

The grounds are lovely: a big rushy lake, bluebells, sunshine, birds and plenty of paths to choose from. I thought I'd done rather well to complete a semi-circle to the back entrance without getting lost, but found it had a cattle grid and no visible gate so I had to go back past the castle and say "mornin'!" to the groundsmen and secret servicemen all over again. Later I chatted to locals who were amazed that I'd been allowed in. I suppose I was such a strange sight that everyone assumed that someone else had given me permission.

I had to follow a boring busy road to Shrule. It was cold and cheerless and Mollie was slow and cheerless after her glimpse of high society. Heavy lorries roared past and a man on a bicycle stopped to say I must be a very wealthy woman. A red pick-up truck loaded with wood screeched to a stop. A tinker got out and said he had a beautiful brown pony at home and how about doing a swap? Heavens, why would I want to swap my lovely white pony for a brown one, even if she does only go at two miles an hour? I declined politely while he asked her age, looked at her teeth, and queried her price. Before leaving he asked, "You waiting long in Ireland?" I had to get him to rephrase it before I understood.

It was easy enough to find Paddy McDonagh in Shrule; I heard a neigh before I saw the forge and found him putting the last shoe on a racehorse. He was straight out of a Real Ireland postcard, with shiny red cheeks, shiny brown eyes, and so strong an accent I could only understand about half his conversation. It didn't matter; it was lovely being in a blacksmith's shop again with the smell of burning hoof and the clutter of old shoes, bits of wrought-iron work, and the ping ping ping of the hammer and whoosh of the flames when the bellows were applied. Paddy took off both Mollie's back shoes and reshaped them so they were less curved on the inside. And he talked. John was right about him being the best blacksmith in Ireland. In fact, in 1959 he was the best in the world, having won an international gold medal against 17 competitors, each the best in their country. His speciality was surgical shoeing, and to win the competition he made 42 different shoes for different

Hilary aged 15 on Tara

Willie Leahy and the
boys bring in a sheep
and her lamb

Willie and me, 2011

Picnic at Aughnanure
Castle, Connemara

The last supper, Clifden

Killary Harbour youth hostel, with Mollie in the garden

Wild camping in Connemara

The daunting hillside in Joyce's Country

John Daly (2011)
'He just oozed
horse magic'

Corcomroe Abbey

Mollie in The Burren

Ireland between the ears –
leaving Killary Harbour

Mountain Aven

The green road between
Doolin and the Cliffs of
Moher

At the Cliffs of Moher

Farmer Tom and
his mum

'Outside was what looked
like a large orange-crate
on wheels'

The final touches
to Mollie's shoes

The O'Shea family

The Valley of the Cows
from the cliff top in 1984
and the same view (inset)
taken in 2011

'"Goodnight Mollie" I called'

hoof problems. He showed me one he'd made for a horse with a foot infection which had pulled its hoof away from all the gooey mess underneath. The shoe was hoof-shaped and he was able to pack it with gauze dressing between the gooey foot and the shoe and attach it with wood screws to the half inch of hoof that was left under the coronet. Nowadays, he said, the apprentices don't want to bother with such skilled work; they expect to buy ready-made shoes. He also showed me a plastic shoe that is being tried out in America but he said they'll never find a substitute for iron. Mollie's shoes looked almost worn down although Paddy said they'd last three more weeks.

He charged me IR£2 for 1½ hours' work, and would take no more. By that time it was after 7 o'clock so I asked him if he knew someone in the village with a field. He suggested the pub down the road and I plucked up courage and knocked at the door.

Chapter 8

It must be alarming to open the door and find yourself face-to-face with an English woman accompanied by a gloomy white horse, but the young girl who answered my knock didn't seem in the least taken aback at my request. She took me to an enormous field of luscious green grass and fresh cow pats next to the pub. Mollie cheered up immediately and I found a good place for my tent in a hollow where I couldn't be seen from the road (I was slightly anxious camping so near to a town). I asked Madeleine if the pub did food (there didn't seem any point in cooking up my meagre soup so near civilisation) and she said she'd make me a sandwich. When I'd got the tent up and Mollie settled, I went to have a Guinness and my sandwich. A group of silent old men stared at me from the bar, but Madeleine brought me through to their living room to serve me a large salad with ham, potatoes, brown bread and coffee. And she would accept no payment. Nor would her mother when she came in. The Hylands were a delightful family. I lost count of how many children but I think it was five; or maybe seven. Or was that the age of the youngest who worked quietly at his homework while we talked?

I had a late start the next day, needing to hitch into Galway to go to the bank (I was still processing the payment to Willie) and to buy some dried meals for my future camp dinners, so it was late afternoon before I was on my way. Riding through the flat countryside beyond Shrule I felt as though I'd ridden into summer. Big fields of summer grass, summer flowers and butterflies and summer smells. The sun was warm on my back as we walked past baaing flocks of newly sheared sheep and I tried to summon the courage to ask for a field for the night. At about 8 o'clock I knew I couldn't procrastinate any longer and stopped a woman walking down the lane. "No, I can't say I know of anywhere," she said rather evasively. An old woman with an arthritic sheepdog was more helpful. "No, sorry, but go back to the two-storey house on the left. They'll help you." The door was opened by the woman I'd stopped in the lane. We were both embarrassed, she explaining that she couldn't say yes without her husband's permission and he was off with the sheep and me apologising and saying I quite understood. She now seemed happy to show me to a large field with plenty of grass, piped water and all mod cons for Mollie and I accepted the offer of a cup of tea once my tent was up. I went to the house in the twilight and found Mum, still apologising, by a table laden with bread and jam, cakes and tea. The rest of the family came in; a newly married couple who were building a house next door, the youngest daughter dressed to the nines for a party, and father who arrived tired from the day's sheep shearing. The television was on with the news of the latest shooting in Northern Ireland. Father turned down the sound decisively and conversation turned to The Situation. "You'll hardly meet anyone who supports the IRA down here. They've set us back a hundred years, they have. Now the English won't come here anymore. It's no good talking about a united Ireland, this just frightens the Protestants. We must win them over slowly. It'll take years but it's the only way." He went on to talk about the Irish Civil War. "'Twas brother against brother. Tragic. When you leave tomorrow, go and look at the cemetery down the road. There are 14 boys buried there who were shot by the Black and Tans and seven who were killed by their own people. 'Tis a desperate shame."

It was raining again in the morning. "Lovely soft morning!" went the greetings. I wouldn't be surprised if the weatherman announced "Lovely soft weather spreading from the West." Mollie was fresh after those acres of green grass and found the road full of life-threatening situations; there was a fierce sparrow, an ominous puddle, a lethal plastic bag, a terrifying flock of geese, a horse-eating terrier, and an ogre of such horrifying aspect that the poor woman had to remove the raincoat held over her head before Mollie would go past.

It rained all day. The scenery was flat and dull, the only excitement being my arrival on a new map. There's always a sense of accomplishment in reaching the edge of a map; it's a destination of sorts in an unplanned journey. I sat hunched in the saddle under my leaking rain cape and listened to Radio 4 on my little transistor while Mollie plodded along with her ears back. She hated the rain – inappropriate, I thought, for a pony born and bred in the west of Ireland. At least there were plenty of farms with large fields, but once again I couldn't bring myself to stop at one until we were both almost dropping with exhaustion. The rain had now cleared and I rode up the driveway to a farmhouse in time for a family crisis. A small child, about two years old, was standing in the track screaming. Facing him was a cow with lowered head and bulging eyes. Behind the cow the child's mother yelled instructions. It was hardly the right moment to make my request so I waited until an older boy had shooed the cow out of the way and led his little sister to safety. Yes, they had a field. It was rather small and scrubby but at least I'd be able to catch Mollie in such a confined area. The farmer's wife said she'd make up a bed for me. "No, no, I'm fine out here," I said, regretting it immediately. But I hated the thought of causing extra work. Besides, I liked the quiet solitude of an evening spent cooking my own meal and writing my diary, with Mollie grazing close by. While unsaddling her I found that she was covered in ticks, so I spent the cocktail hour picking them off with tweezers. Then she found a handy low branch and gave her back a good scratch before kicking over the bucket of water the farmer had kindly brought from the house.

As I packed up the next morning Mollie strolled around waiting for me to notice that she didn't intend to be caught, but by the time I was finished she was bored and allowed me to come up to her and clip the lead rope onto her head collar. That was a sort of break through, but paled beside the event later that day. As always, I had offered her my apple core at lunch time, but this time, instead of turning away disdainfully, she absentmindedly ate it. I laughed out loud at the shocked expression on her face as she chomped it with her lips drawn back and foamy apple juice dripping from her teeth. 'Hey, it's good!' With pricked ears she nuzzled my pocket for more. I stopped at the next shop I came to and wheedled a free carrot out of them. And she ate it. She learned fast, and soon became quite tiresome, stopping dead outside grocery shops and peering into the doorway in the hopes of a handout.

After lunch the flat, monotonous landscape gave way to sea vistas and distant mountains. We were back near Galway Bay with a good view over Dunkellin Estuary and its ruined castle, then open grassland and the dark grey skeleton of a large mansion standing on high ground overlooking the sea. I wondered whether it had been burnt in the Troubles. A few miles down the road I met an elderly man out for a walk. He had an erect posture, a red-veined face, and wore tweeds and two hearing aids. Before he spoke I could guess his accent. "Yes, I can tell you about that ruin. It's Tyrone House. It was built by a black Protestant, Christopher St George. Back in the 1700s. The St Christophers were great huntsmen, you know – they say that one of their horses was buried in a bronze casket. Don't know if that's true, though. Yes, the house was burned by the IRA in the 1920s." He went on to talk about horses. He'd been in the Indian cavalry. "We had 520 horses and mules in each regiment. They were only shod in front, not behind. The hooves soon toughen up, you know." I explained that I was doing too much road work to risk going without shoes, much though I'd love to. "Do you have horses now?" I asked. "I used to, I never stopped riding until just the other day and now I'm too old. Used to hunt three days a week. I did my own horses, too. . . That's a lovely saddle. Army type. They cost a lot of money these days. Very comfortable, ideal for long days in the saddle." Then he raised his hat and wished me good luck. A very charming Horse Protestant.

By taking a circuitous route near the coast I avoided the long stretch of main road to Kinvarra. I had planned to continue to the youth hostel a few miles beyond the town but by 6 o'clock neither Mollie nor I had the will power to go on. It was cold, I badly needed a bath and I thought it was time I treated myself to a B&B. I found a nice-looking place overlooking the harbour with an enclosed grassy area behind a high, locked gate next door. "Would you also have accommodation for my pony?" I asked, indicating the enclosure. "Oh, I should think so. It belongs to the pub so ask Michael." Permission granted. It was pure heaven lying back in a guilt-free hot bath, after consuming numerous cups of tea, with a hot meal to look forward to and knowing that Mollie was safe and happy in an enclosed field. Later I went to the pub to have a Guinness and thank Michael for Mollie's B&B. The bar was very dark, very smoky, and full of men. When I entered, everyone stopped talking and looked at me. I asked if there'd be music that evening and one gave an imperceptible shake of the head and continued staring. So I ordered a Guinness, sat down and drank it very fast, smiling with lowered eyes, then slunk out. The physical dangers of travel are no problem, but pubs are just too frightening.

Well fortified by my comfortable night and satisfyingly greasy breakfast I decided to go in pursuit of literary Ireland. I was carrying in my luggage a slim volume of poetry by Yeats, and learned from my two fellow bed-and-breakfasters, a couple of highly educated American women, that nearby Coole Park was associated with Yeats. "It's a beautiful place. Lovely grounds and the famous Autograph Tree."

"The what?"

"All sorts of literary men carved their initials there." They showed me their guide book: 'The house is in ruins, but the yew walk, garden, woods and autographed copper-beech tree are well kept. Lady Gregory, whose home it was from 1880, was one of the founder members of the Abbey Theatre. One of Yeats's closest friends and literary allies, she immersed herself in Irish traditional life and literature and her house became the centre of literary life in the period.'

I decided to leave my bags at the house and ride like a normal horsewoman to Coole Park (16 miles round trip), then continue on to Doorus House Youth Hostel which completed the Yeats/Lady Gregory connection since the two were introduced there in the days when it was privately owned.

I thought Mollie would be bounding along like a yearling without the saddlebags, but she didn't seem particularly grateful. I was strict with her, however, and did a good amount of fast trotting and cantering which she enjoyed. So did I; she had a lovely comfortable canter. Coole Park was indeed beautiful. Its long tree-lined drive was bordered by forest with inviting woodland trails radiating from it. A pair of friendly hedge-trimmers told me I could ride anywhere I wanted. Tethering Mollie I went to look at the Autograph Tree and eat my lunch in the formal gardens. The huge copper beech stood a little apart from its neighbours, on the fringe of the lawn, its bark deeply inscribed with the initials of the literary giants the period. There's a typically flamboyant GBS (George Bernard Shaw), a subtle SOC for Sean O'Casey, and WBY for Yeats himself.

Later I read about Lady Gregory and liked her. Her rather boring-sounding titled husband at least had the sense to let her follow her enthusiasms; she was a folklorist and a dramatist, and had studied the Irish language from a Bible borrowed from Edward Martyn, a wealthy Catholic landlord. It was he that introduced her to the poet because he couldn't think how to entertain Yeats on a wet afternoon. How satisfying it must have been for Martyn when he saw how well they were getting on and heard their plans for an Irish theatre. To realise the importance of this meeting one must know how uncultured Ireland was in the 19th century. While England was nurturing Dickens and the Brontës, its neighbour, caught in the grip of poverty and famine, was unfruitful. Coole Park became the centre of the literary revival that produced such a high proportion of Irish writers and playwrights at the turn of the century.

After lunch I explored the various trails. Grassy tracks led through woods full of bluebells and pungent with wild garlic; perfect for a gallop except that they were so lovely it seemed a shame not to enjoy it slowly. I did both and managed a serpentine ride that brought me out near the gate.

∩ ∩ ∩

I went back to Coole in 2011 and found it little changed. The woods are still lovely, dark and deep, suffused with the smell of wild garlic, and you can still wander – or ride – for miles along the forest paths or visit the small museum to learn about the former inhabitants. From a distance the Autograph Tree looks the same, its deep maroon colouring standing out among the neighbouring greens, but now it's protected from modern autograph carvers by a fearsome iron railing. The passing years have had surprisingly little effect on the 19th-century initials, but now there is an interpretation sign to help you match the literary figure to the autograph. On my earlier visit I hadn't spotted John M Synge, nor the artist Augustus John who has snuck in there amongst the literati.

∩ ∩ ∩

On the way back to Kinvarra I stopped to visit Lydacan Castle. It was typical of so many Irish ruins, impressive but apparently uncared for, standing lonely in a field full of cows. The solid Norman tower has five floors connected by a spiral staircase. I turned Mollie loose and climbed up to the top, from where I could see the ocean and also Mollie, munching away, surrounded by a surging sea of mooing black and white. Worrying that she might get fed up and kick them, I scampered down again and mounted to return to the road. "Shoo, shoo!" I said feebly at our escort of 20 or so bellowing cattle. But I'd neglected to take any bearings when entering the field, and now that I couldn't see the road I had no idea where it was. Nor had Mollie, I was disgusted to discover. When I dropped the reins and said "Home" she walked briskly back to the castle and started eating.

Back at Kinvarra I succumbed to the offer of a cup of tea, then bagged up and headed for the youth hostel. It was marked on the map but none too accurately, I later realised. A herd of cows was being driven up the lane by an irresponsible sheepdog which took one look at Mollie and fled. The cows scattered and I had to round them up and send them on what I hoped was their way. My way was equally vague; the road dead-ended at a gate opening onto a grassy track. Across the bay I could see a white building which must, I rightly concluded, be Doorus House.

The track led temptingly along the shore towards the hostel, skirting the bay with its glinting blue water. It soon petered out into seaweed, mud and rocks, but it's hard to turn back even after you know you've made a mistake. After all, Doorus House was only just across the bay, the tide was out and the mud/sand looked firm. But a stone wall stood in the way. I didn't think it would be too difficult to take off the top stones and lead Mollie over the lower ones. I dismounted and started heaving the boulders out of the way while Mollie tore ravenously at the scant grass. She stepped over the remaining stones willingly enough and I rebuilt the wall feeling pleased with myself. It was good to use a little initiative at last. I mounted and rode to the mud. Mollie took one step, sank nearly to her knees, and scrambled back onto dry land. Damn, it wasn't going to be easy. But further down I could see where cows had crossed the mud, so saw no reason why Mollie shouldn't be led across. For a while she stood on the edge looking mulish while I hauled on her rope, the mud slurping over the top of my boots. She eventually gave in and we reached the other side with sandy mud sticking to our legs up to the knees. I was now in a field with a herd of cows galloping eagerly up to make our acquaintance. A high stone wall separated us from the road and I could see no gate.

A man sauntered past on the road. "Excuse me," I shouted in some embarrassment, "do you know if there's a gate out of this field?" He looked at me severely. "I don't think so. And farmers won't like you tampering with the walls." He walked on. I was sure they wouldn't, but I was equally sure I wasn't going to retrace my steps. By that time it was 8.30 and I'd phoned the hostel to ask for grazing (yes, it was possible) and said I'd arrive at 7.30. Once the man was out of sight I chose the lowest bit of wall and started dismantling it. The boulders were bigger and heavier than in the earlier wall and the meadow was below the level of the road so that even when I had the top stones off it was not possible for Mollie to step over the large unmoveable lower ones. The best I could do was to reduce the wall to a bank about 2 feet high. I wondered if I could lead Mollie over. She knew I only wondered, that I lacked courage in my convictions, and did her mulish act. I mounted and trotted her at it. She pricked her ears and jumped over without hesitation. I was enormously impressed and pleased with her. I never really believed she would jump with the saddlebags. The grass was certainly greener on the other side which probably helped. She munched while I made a skilful job of rebuilding the wall. I don't think even the beadiest-eyed farmer would have noticed it had been tampered with. I rode up to Doorus House at 9 o'clock feeling very tired, having ridden around 22 miles that day.

"That's an unusual request, you know" said the warden looking at me rather accusingly. "When I said we had grazing I'd forgotten about the weed-killer. You can't tether the pony in front." She paused. "But I'll let you put her in our orchard. It doesn't belong to the hostel but we've been thinking of putting an animal there to keep the grass down."

The orchard was enclosed behind a high wall like Mollie's previous night's lodging, with the same lush grass. This one was like the Secret Garden, approached down a path through head-high cow parsley leading to elegant wrought-iron gates. Once again I could turn Mollie loose to eat her fill and rest after the long day. After I'd removed the saddle she had a vigorous shake and stood haloed in dust and flying white hairs. She was fast losing her winter coat.

I joined the other hostellers in the kitchen to heat my tinned stew and to listen to discussions on where to go next. They seemed to travel so fast – several had been in Killarney the previous night, a place I hoped to reach in two or three weeks. Hitchhiking was easy, they said, but they got tired of answering the same questions again and again, and even tired of drinking Guinness. As a way of meeting people and getting to understand a country, hitchhiking is excellent, but I realised how little these young people saw of the countryside. They had to stick to the main roads, and although many walked several miles a day it was the hitchhikers' walk overlaid with anxieties about the next lift and night's lodging. But they had Ireland at their feet; any part of the country was accessible in a day and the discussion turned to next week's music festival at Ennis. The tourist in me would have liked to go but how could I cavort to music with a pony by my side? And, to be honest, I shrank at the thought of all those drunken crowds. Each day of solitude made it an ever more desirable state.

"Did you see the Burren?" I asked.

"I think so." How could she not be sure? The Burren, described with lyrical enthusiasm by Kieren Guinness, had become one of my goals.

The name describes a type of landscape rather than a clearly defined region, taking its name from Boireann meaning 'a rocky place'. Appropriate enough. From a distance the rounded hills seem to be producing some grey-coloured crop. This is limestone: compressed sand and shells heaved up from the ocean bed and smoothed by glaciation into the characteristic Burren 'paving stones'. It is the youngest landscape in Europe, a treeless world, scoured smooth and clean in the ice age. The Burren is described in images of death. As William Trevor in his irresistible book *A Writer's Ireland* puts it, 'The very bones of Ireland's landscape break through its skin on the Burren', and Cromwell's surveyors described it as 'yielding neither water enough to drown a man, nor a tree to hang him, nor soil enough to bury him'.

A good map, one inch to the mile, hung on the hostel wall, the first Ordnance Survey one I'd seen in this scale. It was only in black and white but showed all sorts of possibilities missing on my smaller-scale maps. I bemoaned to the warden the difficulty of getting decent maps. "It's for security reasons. Suppose the Russians got hold of them!"

Chapter 9

The morning was perfect. Sunny and clear; much too beautiful for me to leave the coast without some further exploring. The large-scale map in Doorus House had suggested that I could ride west along a beach for a couple of miles, so I set out eagerly, longing for a gallop along sand. But this wasn't really a beach. Mollie's hooves sank into the shingle, slipped on the rocks, and skidded on the seaweed. I dismounted and led her over the surf-smoothed pebbles, content to amble along watching the changing light on the sea while Mollie shoved me in the back with her nose.

We left the coast at a small, sheltered cove and followed a narrow lane inland. Ahead were the grey domed hills of the Burren, with Abbey Hill the most easterly bump on the horizon, and there was the green road that I'd spotted on the map, contouring the side of the hill. I found it easily and my heart lifted to hear the soft print of Mollie's hooves on turf instead of the clip-clop of iron on tarmac. Ahead, between her pricked ears, was the curve of the hill, with the sun glinting on the wet limestone, and to the right, beyond the bay, the blue mountains of Connemara where I'd started my trek 10 days ago. The Burren seems to grow boulders instead of crops; to produce food, or even grazing, the farmers have to pick up every stone, by hand,

and create a wall. So the fields are tiny and the walls are many, for what can you do with all those stones except make a wall?

Back on the coastal road, at Bell Harbour, a sign pointed to Corcomroe Abbey. Yeats had set his one-act play *The Dreaming of the Bones* here, a place where 'even the sunlight can be lonely'. I decided to take a look. The abbey is still as lonely as the sunlight which bathes the ruins. Small ferns have found footing on the walls and wild flowers grow in profusion around the graves. Even the incongruous plaster Jesus with its plastic flowers has its place here, a modern expression of devotion which has prevailed over 800 years. The Cistercians built this place early in the 12th century, a massive undertaking in such a remote spot. Where did they find the stonemasons to carve those human and dragon heads which adorn one of the arches? They called the abbey St Mary of the Fertile Rock, revealing that these Burren valleys produced sufficient food for a large religious community.

Near the abbey is a small, ruined house abutting a meadow. The gate was open so I decided to let Mollie have a proper lunch break, untethered and without the luggage, while I ate my picnic nearby. I unbuckled the little straps that linked her bit to the head collar, and she plunged her head down to graze while I unfastened the saddlebags and heaved them onto the ground and took off the saddle. It made a convenient back rest while I ate my sandwiches and watched Mollie tearing up mouthfuls of grass. Later I wandered through the peaceful ruins, taking in the elegant Romanesque arches and the carved foliage atop the capitals. And the effigies; staring upwards with a pained expression was Conor O'Brien, grandson of Donal Mor O'Brien, the King of Munster who founded the abbey. More serene is an ecclesiastical gentleman with a massive folded tunic and a dinky little mitre, and the smiley face surrounded by flower petals could have come from a modern greetings card.

My map showed a path running across the saddle that lies south of Moneen mountain, suggesting a perfect short cut to Ballyallaban where

I hoped to find a field for Mollie with a horse-breeder friend of John Daly's. Perhaps this would be another green road. As I rode up a narrow lane serving a few farms, I kept scanning the hills in front of me. I could see the saddle between the two peaks but no sign of a track. A new road had been cut into the limestone, just wide enough to take a tractor, but it ran in the wrong direction. At the last farm I dismounted, tied Mollie to the gate, and went for advice.

A tangle of children came to the door, giggling and hiding behind each other. It seemed that the road was the only way, and never mind that it went steeply up hill and south, not west. Mollie puffed and panted and I felt sorry for her, and dismounted. I puffed and panted and finally, after climbing about 800ft, reached the top to find a desolate view of barren rocky hills with no sign of habitation. The road even managed to climb higher. Before I got to the true summit the clouds closed in and swathes of mist obscured the view. We plodded on and on, downhill when possible, at each break in the clouds hoping to see the valley. It started to rain.

I was lost, and fed up. I'd give up on Ballyallaban, set up camp, and hope the weather would improve. I always had enough dried food for the odd night of wild camping, but both Mollie and I needed water. I found a food trough which had a little rainwater in the bottom but, needless to say, Mollie wouldn't go near it, despite my loud and eloquent arguments.

Scooped out of the grey hillside was a good campsite, protected on three sides by cliffs, with flat places for the tent and decent grass for Mollie. Perhaps I could risk not tethering her. Under the cliffs was a small copse of stunted hazel trees with dead branches lying around. I heaved them through the rain and made a reasonable barrier, finishing the effect with Mollie's tether rope. It was only an effect, she could have easily pushed her way through or even stepped over, but I hoped she'd take the hint. I remembered a man on Willie's trek telling me "At best a fence is only a request." A horse, he said, could jump virtually anything – if it wanted to. I needed water for cooking so took my plastic bucket and drinking cup back to the rain-filled food trough. The water was full of debris but otherwise clean and I scooped it up into the bucket. While I cooked my rather meagre soup dinner inside the tent I could hear Mollie chomping the lush grass outside.

In the Burren, farmers drive their cattle up to the highlands during the winter so they can feed in these grassy hollows. It's the reverse of the practice in other parts of Europe where cows are brought down from the mountains in winter to the valleys when the first snows appear. But climatically the Burren is the reverse of other mountainous areas: here the temperature is actually warmer on the hillsides and grass grows well throughout the winter so cattle need no extra feed. The limestone acts as a storage heater, absorbing warmth during the day, so the temperatures rarely drop below freezing at night.

I was uneasy in the tent that night, concerned that Mollie might make her escape and head back to Connemara. While it was still light I kept the tent door open so I could see her, and after dark I listened for her blowing her nose, a comforting horsey sound. The rain pattered gently on the fly sheet all night and at 6 the next morning I put on my glasses, unzipped the door and looked out at her blurry white dozing figure, dripping in the mist. I liked early mornings in the tent. On my own I had no reason to pretend that this is the best time of day, nor that the sounds of nature were preferable to the BBC. I switched the radio on and snoozed through the stock reports, *Yesterday in Parliament*, and other gloriously faraway subjects. It was still raining when the 7 o'clock news came on, and still raining at 8. I thought I'd better get up anyway. I still couldn't cope with the guilt of staying in my sleeping bag half the day, sensible though it might have been.

Mollie was particularly tiresome that morning. There was nowhere to tie her and she kept walking away with a determined expression on her face while I followed her, soaking my boots in the wet grass and cursing her in tender tones. The rain seemed set for the day, falling through a thick mist, and I knew I would have to steer by compass. I was completely lost but it didn't seem to matter; I knew the lane would lead somewhere. Eventually.

As we crossed from one farmer's land to another, gates barred our way. The first was a challenge: the catch was stiff, the wind blew my rain cape over my face, and Mollie jibbed. I hated dismounting in the rain. Not only did the saddle get wet but my carefully arranged limbs let in the water. By the eighth gate Mollie had learned her job and co-operated fully. It's not difficult to open a gate from a horse's back as long as it doesn't run backwards just as you're pulling the catch up.

The lane kept dividing, but using the compass I chose the forks to the west and eventually, two hours after leaving the campsite, dropped steeply downhill, passing some new barns which suggested that I was reaching civilisation. A black figure with two dripping sheepdogs appeared out of the mist and stared at me in astonishment. I asked him if we were near the road. "Sure but you are, there's a gate just down there. But 'tis locked," he added as an afterthought. "Ye'll get over the wall," he said comfortingly and went on his way. You bet I will, I thought grimly. I wasn't about to retrace my steps to the farm with the giggling children. The gate was indeed padlocked. I tied Mollie to it and cast around for a low section of the wall to dismantle. I didn't have to look far, the top stones were missing and the lower ones were easily removed to make a gap that Mollie could step over.

I didn't really know where I was but guessed it was not far above Ballyallaban. The rain continued to fall steadily, driven by the blustery wind. Mollie hated it and walked with her head almost touching the ground, and her face turned sideways away from the wind. She looked silly, like a peevish camel, and I pulled her head up when cars approached. Despite – or perhaps because of – my rain gear, everything was wet: my boots, trousers, arms (the seams of my jacket leaked), hair. I sat hunched in the saddle and even passed by a sign to the dolman tomb which I knew I wanted to see. I was too wet to dismount.

I had to get off when I reached the entrance to Ballyallaban and a cattle grid. Some cement-filled barrels blocked the gap in the wall that provided the only access for Mollie and me. Behind them, among the cows, I could see a chunky black bull. Keeping an eye on it, I pulled the middle barrel towards me and the pool of rain lying on top of the concrete sloshed over the remaining dry part of my trousers. The bull raised its head. I nervously led Mollie into the field and hauled the barrel across the gap again. The bull watched placidly while I remounted and then continued grazing.

The house seemed closed up. There were no cars in the drive, the curtains were drawn, and no barking dogs rushed out at me. I wondered what to do. I felt too wet and depressed to continue riding, and too wet and depressed to find somewhere else to camp. Mollie didn't share my feelings; she had seen other horses and her head was up and her eyes bright with anticipation. I tied her to a dripping chestnut tree and, without any hope, rang the doorbell. I was quietly shocked when I heard footsteps and the door was opened by a young woman who interrupted my prepared statement with "Oh hello, we've been expecting you, do come in."

Mary soon cleared up the mystery. John Daly had visited the family a few days earlier and told them I might turn up. I stood and dripped in the porch and Mary suggested I spend the rest of the day there and stay the night. "You can turn the mare loose out here," (you can always tell genuinely horsey people – they talk in terms of geldings and mares) "and dry your things by the fire." Better and better. It was a marvellous old-fashioned kitchen with a huge fireplace and hooks above the range for suspending kettles and pots and giant hooks on the high black ceiling for hanging bacon. Mary bustled around with admirable energy, finishing off the cleaning while I attempted to converse with Dad, who sat with his head in his hands by the fire. I had every sympathy. Why would he want to chat to a strange, sodden Englishwoman? I watched the steam rise from my clothes, while trying not to stare at Dad's attire. He was dressed in threadbare corduroys and a manure-coloured tweed jacket whose sleeve was making a bid for independence. Just a few threads still connected it to the main.

"I thought I'd hitch into Kilfenora this afternoon," I told Mary when she joined me by the fire. "The cathedral is interesting, isn't it? And the Burren Centre?"

"Oh, I'll drive you in – there are some messages I have to get." I must have looked puzzled. "You know – groceries." We sat down to an enormous lunch which I devoured with my usual greed, gushing my appreciation between mouthfuls, and then Mary drove me to Kilfenora via a roundabout route so I could see some of the Burren in the clearing weather. Strange to be in a car again and cover 20 miles in half an hour instead of a day. I thought what a waste it would be to do all your Irish sightseeing like that.

I described my visit to Kilfenora Cathedral in a letter home:

The cathedral is as usual, in ruins (not surprising, it was built around 1190). It has some nice carvings, but these are nothing compared with the Doorty Cross, which is what I most wanted to see. It's in the churchyard, set around with the usual vulgar modern gravestones, and of typical Celtic design but carved with the most imaginative pictures. None of the descriptions I've read tells you what they're of, except the 'Entrance into Jerusalem' on one side, so I'll give you my interpretation. Well, the entrance into Jerusalem is fairly straightforward if you accept that the donkey is either wearing size 13 wellingtons or has sea lion flippers not legs, and that Jesus's upper body has completely disappeared in holy squiggles and curlicues. It's a bit weathered at the top, near the cross part, so it's hard to see just what is going on, but the other side, protected from the prevailing wind, is clear enough. Except that I still don't understand it. There's a figure wearing a rather trendy embroidered tunic and a glum expression. He's sporting the same dunce's cap that Donal Thor O'Brien wears in Corcomroe Abbey so perhaps it's a Celtic version of a bishop's mitre. Except that his expression fits a dunce better than a bishop. In his left had he hold a curly-topped crozier, while two parrots use his shoulders as springboards. This holy man is standing on the heads of two faceless hooded characters that maybe have their arms entwined or maybe the Celtic carver just gave way to his curlicue yearnings. They're also holding staffs with which they're prodding the creature below them. Impossible to say what this is – a dragon, maybe? Or a griffin? It's got two legs, anyway, and is standing on a pair of skulls. Or perhaps urns. All in all there's a lot going on.

In 2003 the Doorty Cross was moved to a new, less atmospheric, position under cover. And cleaned up, so more detail is exposed and it's lost some of its mystery. I'm glad I saw it in 1984 when imagination could take flight.

Mary dropped me off at one of the few established tourist sites in the Burren. Ailwee cave is a long, deep, heavily commercialised limestone cave with a few stalagmites, stalactites and claw marks from bears. Also on display were the antlers of one of my favourite extinct animals, the Irish elk, designed while God was going through his Celtic curlicue period. And I learned that the last Irish wolf was killed at the end of the 18th century in Co Sligo. So sheep may safely graze, and wolfhounds have become redundant. I've only seen one Irish wolfhound in Ireland; it was sitting morosely outside a pub in Dublin.

I woke to one of those lovely washed mornings with a green/blue sky and birds singing from every tree. Mollie had been turned out in the huge field with the brood mares so I wondered if I'd be able to catch her. No problem, by the time I'd finished breakfast Mary already had her tied up outside the house, and I was able to groom her using a proper dandy brush instead of my mail-order pet brush with retractable bristles that didn't really work. I loved grooming Mollie, running my hands over the curve of her shoulder and along her back, pulling burrs out of her mane and brushing all the mud and manure out of her thick, long tail. I loved the soft, folded skin between her front legs and the way the dapples on her quarters were emerging now she was shedding her thick winter coat. By the time I had finished there was a heap of white hair on the ground and she looked sleek and summery. As always I checked her back for sores and picked out her hooves. Her shoes were looking increasingly worn but I reckoned they'd last another couple of weeks before I needed to find a blacksmith.

Mollie was in an obliging mood; the half-day's rest in aristocratic company had obviously done her a world of good. Perhaps she'd enjoyed boasting about her exploits:

"I come from Connemara."

"That's nothing, I was born in Tipperary."

"Bet you got here in a horse box."

"Well, how else are you going to travel?"

"I came on hoof."

"You mean you *walked* all the way from Connemara?"

Mary and I peered at the map spread over the kitchen table while I munched my last bit of brown bread. Ballyallaban House was there, and I could see my route down into the valley then up to Feenagh. "See that green road? It'll take you over the col to Formoyle and you should be able to get across the hills on that track." This is now the Burren Way, but in 1984 it was just a speculative route on the map, made all the more seductive by its uncertainty.

The track was rough and stony, with yesterday's puddles still lying in the ruts. At the top of the pass the view was so perfect, and the sun so warm,

I decided to have a long lunch break and again undress Mollie completely so we both could relax for an hour. There was no-one around except a man on a tractor who came to pass the time of day and admire my pony. I loved it when people asked "Where did you hire the horse?" and I could say "She's mine!" After I'd eaten my home-baked bread and marmite I left Mollie to graze and wandered around photographing flowers. My information booklet told me that the Burren is a meeting place of flowers from northern and southern Europe. It is thought that before the last ice age this area had a warm climate and southern plant species flourished, then seeds from the north arrived trapped in the glaciers – along with boulders and other debris – which spread over the Burren. When the ice receded it scraped and smoothed the limestone hills and left a mixture of northern and southern plants. 'There is nowhere in Europe where Mediterranean and Arctic-alpine plants grow together in a similar way.'

Early purple orchids were still in flower and plentiful, and between the boulders, clumps of primroses, celandine, and delicate mountain avens brought splashes of yellow and cream, along with magenta from bloody cranesbill and the pure blue of gentians. While I was looking for flowers I wandered over the limestone paving stones. These are quite extraordinary. They run in fluted dimpled rows with deep gaps separating them. The gaps, grykes, run pedantically from north to south, and I could just imagine God with his compass and spirit level laying out this huge rock Garden of Eden and getting so carried away with the civil engineering he forgot that apple trees won't grow here (nor snakes, come to that).

From my lunch spot I could see a track running between stone walls over the opposite hillside. Mary had thought it might be blocked by a wall but my binoculars showed it to be clear at least to the col.

As we dropped down to the Caher valley I spotted a couple of walkers gazing at the turbulent river. The two women told me they were from

Ulster and holidayed regularly in the Republic. "Splendid, splendid! What a marvellous thing you're doing! No, we haven't been all the way to the top, but the path's clear for the first part. No wall." A grove of stunted hazel trees partially blocked the entrance to the track, but Mollie and I pushed our way through and panted up the steep hill. Stone walls ran on either side of the track, the flat boulders placed on their edges to create a filigree design. Stone walls encircled fields of stones, and ran up the grey limestone hillsides in long, wavy lines.

There was indeed a wall at the top of the pass, but it was hardly an obstruction; I could easily make a gap for Mollie to step over, and after that it was simply glorious – a wide grassy track where I could canter whenever I, or Mollie, felt like it. And, obviously thrilled to be off the tarmac, she felt like it. Even at a gallop she seemed able to ignore the bouncing saddlebags. Sometimes it was too beautiful to gallop; the sky was full of larks, flowers lined the track and the grey domes of the Burren contrasted with rugged blue hills to the south – the mountains of Kerry! My next destination seemed a long, long way away, but so did the bens of Connemara where I'd started from.

After that first wall, there were no obstructions apart from an occasional gate. The track ran high on the flanks of Slieve Elva, a hill quite out of keeping with the Burren, with incongruous conifers and a shale summit, before dropping down to farms and tiny, stone-walled fields on the road to Doolin – 17 miles of perfect riding.

Chapter 10

I wanted to spend the night in Doolin because everyone kept telling me that this is the centre for Irish music, but the glories of that day in the Burren had wiped all practical thoughts from my mind. So when I rode past a 'Hostel' sign it took me a while to register that this was a Good Thing; I turned round and rode back again, tied Mollie outside, and went to look for the warden. Up until then I'd stayed in a few YHA places, but this was the first independent hostel I'd seen, although I'd been told they were more relaxed than the official places with fewer rules and a wider variety of users: couples and older people. People like me, in fact.

There was no accommodation for Mollie and the Australian girl looking after the place didn't know of anyone with a field. "You'll have to ask around the village. I'll keep an eye on the pony." First I enquired in a rather raucous pub and they all said ask Mr Brown, then fell about laughing. So I found Mr Brown who was lurking behind a cottage, so run down it was almost indistinguishable from the surrounding countryside; the walls were sprouting plants and most of the thatched roof seemed to have reverted to mud and grass. Mr Brown was also sprouting. Poor man, he had some awful infection on his pendulous lower lip. Having found him, I felt I'd better press on with my request but I never found out if he had a field since I couldn't understand what he said. It seemed unlikely, so I thanked him profusely and left. My next effort was a farm surrounded by well-fenced fields. A group of men were cutting silage so I walked up and asked them if I could graze my pony in one of the fields. They told me to check with a large woman who was standing rather vaguely in the farmyard. She stood with her hands on her hips, looking at me out of one eye while the other wandered over the surrounding hills. "Well, I'm not sure. . . the calves wouldn't like it, they've never seen a horse. . . no, I don't think so." I tried hard to persuade her that Mollie was indifferent to other animals, had spent plenty of nights with cows, and needed somewhere secure for just one night. "No, I don't think so." So I gave up. I'd spotted a grassy area by the river as I rode to the hostel and had thought at the time that this would do at a pinch. I tethered Mollie close to the bridge where she could reach water to drink as well as the grass. But I worried about her incessantly as I cooked and ate my supper. Suppose she was stolen by tinkers or molested by the children?

The hostel was almost deserted, but the few people there were in Doolin for the music. A Swiss girl and I headed off to the pub that's reputed to have the best players, and already there were more visitors than locals. The music was excellent – if you like traditional Irish music. I realised I don't. I like everything about it except the actual sound. I like the old toothless cloth-capped men playing tin whistles, the younger equally toothless boys playing fiddles, the atmosphere, and the fact that the tradition of Irish music is alive and well and – from what I was told by a music group in Dublin – played for pleasure, not just for tourists, but. . . not the music itself. So I left after an hour or so and made my way back down the pitch-dark lanes, getting lost in the process, and finally coming to Mollie's bridge and stumbling down the bank to give her a goodnight kiss.

I was up horribly early to check on her. She was fine, which was more than could be said for the weather. I found a phone box and called the recorded weather forecast. "Rain clearing by noon," they said, so I moved Mollie's tether and left her to have a leisurely breakfast, while I sat in the warm, dry common room, writing letters and planning the next stage of my journey.

'A great, undulating wall of rock.' That's how my guidebook described the Cliffs of Moher; nearly 700 feet high, they were obviously a major tourist attraction since even the girl who wasn't sure if she'd seen the Burren was quite certain she'd been to the Cliffs of Moher and that they were spectacular. And even better, my map showed a green road running close to the sea between Doolin and the highest point, O'Briens's Tower.

As I was riding up the hill out of the village, a tourist coach drew up behind me and its occupants jumped out to take pictures. I wonder how their guide explained this quintessentially Irish scene? One particularly large lady panted along the other side of the road trying to get a photo from the front; by the time she'd got her camera focussed I was too close and she had to run ahead again. This happened several times until I softened and stopped for her – which I would have done at the beginning had she, or her fellow passengers, spoken to me.

We soon left the tarmac to follow a classic green road, skirting the shore and rising steeply ahead to hug the cliffs. It was even lovelier than yesterday; the wide track followed an inadequate fence that kept cattle and Mollie from the cliff's edge where pink thrift grew in clumps over pockets of green sea, and sea birds were speckled white against the black rock. I gave Mollie a break while I sat on the cliff edge with my binoculars, identifying great black-backed gulls, fulmars, terns, and guillemots while a couple of choughs wheeled overhead shouting 'ch-ang!'

This beautiful old road continued for about a mile with only views to delay me. The first river was crossed by an ancient stone bridge but the track stopped at the next stream which had cut its way through the pasture to the sea in a deep channel, bridged by a single wooden plank. I dismounted and considered my options. The river banks were about five feet deep and white water cascaded between large boulders. Impossible. A path of sorts veered off to the right, following the stream, so I led Mollie along it looking for a crossing place. Frustratingly there was a ford that had obviously been used by cattle, but beyond it the fields separating us from the resumption of the track were divided by three high and solid stone walls. Leaving Mollie to graze I took a close look at these. The first two were well built with huge boulders and the last had a gap, but blocked with a plank piled with gargantuan stones. I couldn't get through that way. I turned my attention to the river. Perhaps if I cleared the boulders Mollie could be persuaded to jump down the bank into the water and scramble up the other side. There was a place where the drop was only about three feet. I heaved the boulders to the side and made an inviting landing pad at the bottom. "Come on Mollie!" She dug her feet in and looked down in horror. "It's only a little jump," I said, pulling her. No go. I slid down the bank and hauled pointlessly on her lead rope. She stood firmly on the bank three feet above me, leaning back against the rope. I felt like a climber scaling a rock face and cursed Mollie's chin; she looked particularly irritating from that angle. Climbing up the bank again I mounted and rode her at it. When we got to the edge my nerve gave out. Of course she was right! It was a stupid thing to attempt. I apologised, let her get on with her eating, and heaved the rocks back into their original position.

Perhaps the area by the bridge would be easier. There was a boulder-free bit of bank she could descend safely, then a short walk down the river bed, and up the other side. It was worth trying. I spent ages preparing the way, taking down the bridge, clearing the riverbed, but Mollie wasn't having any of it. She was becoming fed up with my ambitions; while I reconstructed

the bridge she tried to sneak back to Doolin. The only possible course
(apart from returning the way I had come which was unthinkable) was to
try to get over the walls.

Leading Mollie over the ford to a new patch of grass, I started lifting
the top stones off the first wall. They were very heavy and I found that rock
dropped on rock with a finger in between hurts. There was no question of
removing the lower boulders – they were much too large – so I was left
with a three-foot-high wall. It was jumpable but higher than anything we'd
attempted before. It was worth a try. I cleared the approach and landing area
of rocks and stones, mounted and rode up to the wall so Mollie could look at
it and see what was expected of her. Then I pushed her into a canter and she
jumped it without hesitation. I was thrilled! It must be harder for a horse to
jump with an extra 40-pound dead weight; I wondered if she'd be less willing
to do the next wall. She trotted up with pricked ears and popped over. What
a splendid pony I had for this job! She was too sensible to agree to my doing
anything dangerous. All that was left now was to clear the giant stones from
the plank blocking the last gap. They were huge, but by this point I just had
to move them, and after I'd passed through I had to put them back again. As
with all the walls, I had to try to leave them exactly as I found them.

My relief at being back on the track was short-lived. There was another
wall; smaller stones this time, but with a strand of barbed wire along the
top. This I was able to unloop and pull back. And so it went on: between the
stream and the end of the green road there were eight fences. Some were
straightforward walls, others were fiendishly complicated wire fences with
a dozen spiky strands to be untwined, or a combination of stone and wire.
One took me half an hour to deal with but by this time I'd reached the
point of no return; I couldn't bear the thought of undoing all those fences
I'd so carefully reassembled behind me. I dreaded meeting one that couldn't
be taken down or undone.

Eventually I could hear traffic and see it racing along the main road. The track rose towards it, skirting the edge of a large ploughed field. I could see the final gate opening onto the road and prayed hard that it wouldn't be padlocked. Two farmers were walking slowly through the field, deep in discussion. Would they tell me off for trespassing? I gave them a cheery greeting as I rode up to the gate which, to my immense relief, was easily opened and I passed through to the main road.

I had ridden a little over four miles that morning; it had taken me just under four hours.

"Hello!" A suntanned girl, on a bike loaded with luggage, greeted me enthusiastically. "Oh, that is so good! I have a horse in Switzerland." We discussed the relative merits of horse versus bicycle but of course it was no contest. She longed to do what I was doing, and I enjoyed answering her questions. I was proud of my gear, the distance I'd covered (about 300 miles so far) and of course my pony. I told her about all the fences and walls, and how Mollie jumped them. And I showed her the two swollen fingers which would soon develop black nails where I'd dropped the stones. And I stroked Mollie's neck in appreciation.

I wondered what it would have been like travelling with a companion. It had been a tough day, full of anxiety, the sort of day that would have been merely an adventure with someone to share it. But although a trouble shared is a trouble halved, it's not the same with beauty. I'm not sure that my spirits would have soared to the same heights if I had discussed those sea views with a friend.

A number of coaches passed me as I rode up to the Cliffs of Moher Information Centre, a small white building perched on a grassy hill, and I soon found myself surrounded by excited Americans and clicking cameras. One girl was overcome. "Oh my, this has just made my whole trip! I can't believe it!" It was cold and windy, I'd eaten an early and inadequate lunch, so I thought a cup of tea and a few cakes in the tearoom would slip down a treat. There was excellent grazing for Mollie outside, so I led her up to the highest part of the hill, away from the path, screwed the picket into the ground and tethered her from the head collar; the hobble was too deep in my saddlebags. I sipped my tea and wrote postcards, half listening to other visitors discussing a white horse in excited voices. Then, with rain threatening, I went out to look at the cliffs, leaving Mollie eating her tea on the hillside.

The Cliffs of Moher are indeed impressive, but not, I thought, as beautiful as the cliffs I'd gazed at earlier that morning nor those of a similar height in Aran. Few tourist sights can retain their impact when the viewpoints are crowded with visitors. However, I learned that Mollie and I were perhaps lucky when we visited the more dramatic cliffs to the north. They are not horse-friendly. The Irish name is *Aill Na Searrach*, which translates as The Cliff of the Foals. Many, many years ago, they say, Ireland was ruled by the Tuatha Dé Danann. Perhaps they were kings, or maybe gods, for they arrived on a cloud and had magic powers. One king feared for his daughters, that they might be taken by his enemies, so he shut them in a cave in Kilcornan. Years went by before the girls, understandably frustrated by their incarceration, transformed themselves into young horses – foals – and burst from the cave. Dazzled by the unaccustomed light they galloped blindly to the west, towards the setting sun, towards the sea, to the very edge of the Cliffs of Moher where they leapt to their death. But the force is still with them, or with those cliffs. In 2004, surfers discovered Ireland's greatest wave at the foot of these very cliffs. It is popularly known as Aileen's Wave, a corruption of *Aill Na Searrach*.

I was the only person venturing along the cliff path, most being content to climb up to the viewpoint and take their photos. I wanted to look for puffins which are said to build their burrows in the cliffs. There were plenty of other sea birds and I was sitting happily with my binoculars spotting kittiwakes and guillemots when I saw something out of the corner of my eye. Something white. Mollie was in difficulties. I was too far away to see clearly, but I could tell what had happened. Her rope had become wound round her back leg and by struggling she had not only made it tighter but it was pulling her head between her forelegs. It all seemed to happen in slow motion – I watched appalled as she battled the rope until something broke and she was sent cart-wheeling down the hill; the rounded bulk of the saddlebags over her back and sides made her almost circular. When she reached the bottom Mollie got to her feet and continued grazing as though this was a perfectly normal method of descent. By that time I was running towards her with mingled dread and relief; she obviously wasn't badly hurt but would I find her lame? "She's fine, don't worry," said the man holding her rope. In fact Mollie seemed much less shaken by the incident than I was, although I suppose it's difficult to see if a white horse has turned pale. I walked her around and she was indeed fine; the saddlebags hadn't even slipped, so I rode her up to O'Brien's Tower and asked a German tourist to take our photo. Then I left the cliffs and headed south for Lehinch where I was to pick up my mail.

∩ ∩ ∩

In 2007 the Cliffs of Moher had a makeover. The little information centre on Mollie's grassy cart-wheel slope has been replaced by The Cliffs of Moher Experience, created inside the hillside, and hordes of tourists pay their €6 to enter and marvel at the cliffs from behind safety barriers. However, by the time you read this, a new path will have opened following most of the route that I took with Mollie, but without the walls and without the ankle-deep bog that I squelched through on my return visit in 2011. It will continue beyond the Cliffs of Moher, via Hag's Head, to Liscannor, a walk of 14 kilometres. And it will be wonderful!

∩ ∩ ∩

Mollie and I walked along narrow lanes past large fields. Silage cutters were out in force, the lush green grass being scooped up by giant machines and transported to the farmyard to mature. The evening sun slanted through the grass giving it that peculiarly Irish glow. In the tropics I was used to seeing the sun shine directly over the landscape, giving a flat shadowless look to the scenery, at least at noon. Here the sun was always low, and in the evening, when it was just above the horizon, it shone through the vegetation and even blades of grass were lit from behind. Then the grey clouds blew across the sun and the first spots of rain began to fall. I pulled on my rain chaps (no need to dismount to do this) and got out my yellow cycling cape. It poured. Huge chilly drops of rain slammed against us. Mollie put her head down, ears back and face sideways, away from the wind, her whole posture expressing misery at being subjected to such discomfort. We passed a farmyard with a large hay barn. The door was slightly open and I could see the farmer working inside. On impulse I turned into the yard, the farmer pulled back the sliding door and Mollie and I walked inside out of the rain. I didn't quite know what to say, but it wasn't necessary to say anything. The farmer helped me off with the saddlebags, and I asked if Mollie could spend the night in one of his fields. And perhaps I could sleep in the barn? No problem. I was rather pleased. In books, people often sleep in hay barns, but I'd never managed it before. The rain stopped as suddenly as it had started and I put Mollie into the field with some calves and a donkey.

The farmer got on with mending a fence and I went for a walk to dry off and fill in a bit of time. I was near the village of Liscannor, and could see the white houses of Lehinch across the curved, sandy bay, picked out by the setting sun. A few yards from my barn I came to a sign announcing an independent hostel half a mile away. What a temptation! A hot shower, company and a comfortable bunk. I stared at the sign and pondered. I didn't really want to talk to anyone, nor make the effort of sorting through my saddlebags for the items I'd need for a night there. I turned away from the sign and walked along the road to the beach. The tide was out, which meant it would be low in the morning so I should be able to take Mollie along the sands to Lehinch. I crossed a mini rubbish dump and trod down some rusty barbed wire which made a half-hearted attempt to block access to the beach. The bay was patterned with wavy ridges of hard sand and trapped sea water reflecting the evening sky. Flocks of redshanks and dunlin waded in the shallows near the river which bisected the bay, and oyster catchers picked around the smooth pebbles. I was glad I hadn't gone to the hostel.

Back in the barn I prepared my bed for the night by spreading the unfolded tent over a nice heap of straw and rolling around until I'd made a hollow for my sleeping bag. Then I found a large flat stone for my candle. I knew I shouldn't even think about lighting a candle in a hay barn but since I had to have light I would just have to be very careful. I found a plank of wood as a base for the cooking stove and filled my bucket from a water butt. It was wiggling with mosquito larvae. No bath tonight; I wasn't even going to undress. Then I sat on a hay bale near the door, in the fading light, and wrote my diary, measured my mileage (only nine) and planned the next day's route. And felt chilly and lonely. But I managed not to set fire to the barn. It was a comfortable bed, and I slept well. When I packed up the next day I found the nice fresh straw I thought I'd been sleeping on was impregnated with cow dung and that my legs were covered with itchy bites.

Mollie walked up to me with a little whicker, and nuzzled in my pocket for a titbit. Gone were the days of chasing her around the field in the morning. I had her groomed, watered, saddled and bagged by 8 o'clock and set off for Lehinch before the farmer was up, leaving a thank-you note in the barn. Mollie stepped over the rusty barbed wire onto the dunes leading to the beach and quickened her step in anticipation of a gallop. It was the first time I'd ridden her on sand since that first day by Omey Island, but I was content to walk and look at the morning light on the ribbed sand and the surf, and the wading birds. I took out my binoculars but bird watching on horseback is not satisfactory; I could never convince Mollie of the importance of keeping still. We came to the river and Mollie gazed at it with bulging eyes and a 'You cannot be serious!' snort. I saw no reason for such a fuss, considering she'd actually swum with me in Connemara, so urged her on vigorously. Reluctantly she waded in to the deep fast water in the centre. Here the riverbed was composed of slippery seaweed-covered stones and the water swirled well above her knees and splashed over my boots. Halfway, though. Silly to go back at this point. I kept up my encouragement, Mollie kept up her snorts of complaint, and we emerged the other side with mutual expressions of relief. There was still a mile of firm sand between the river and Lehinch and I urged Mollie into a gallop, kicking up chunks of sand and scattering the gulls. Can anyone gallop on a beach without grinning euphorically? I know I can't. It's a wonderful feeling. Then the cheese-'n'-chutney roll bag thudded to the ground because I hadn't secured it properly and I had to pull up, dismount and fret over my camera.

I rode down Lehinch's high street just as the shops were opening. Having skipped breakfast, I planned to collect my mail and have a cup of coffee, so found an out-of-the-way telegraph pole to tie Mollie to. Hearing the hoof beats, a woman peered out of a door near my selected tethering post. "I'll throw an eye on her," she said, when I explained that I was going to be gone a while. "You go and have a good breakfast." A good breakfast

– why not? I deserved it. The tiny post office had a couple of poste restante letters for me and I asked the girl behind the counter to recommend a place that would serve a decent breakfast. The Atlantic Hotel did look a bit posh, but I went in anyway. The receptionist looked at me in disgust and, not trusting herself to speak, nodded in the direction of the dining room. A loo was the first priority. Catching myself in the mirror I thought the receptionist's expression of distaste was quite generous: my nose was peeling, I had straw in my hair, sand on my boots, spurs on my heels, horse grime on my baggy trousers, grease on my cheese-'n'-chutney roll bag cum shoulder bag, and purple patches on my fingernails from wall building. I looked dreadful. I tried to enter the dining room with poise and dignity, easing my way round the tables of staring tourists, and ordered a huge breakfast from surly waiters in red jackets that matched the tablecloths. The food was uninspiring and I thought again how lucky I was in my chosen mode of travel, never normally having to pay so much for so little. I read my mail then studied the map.

Lehinch marked the end of the Burren and the most interesting part of Co Clare. Had I been a normal tourist I would have motored to the Killimer–Tarbert car ferry across the Shannon, and been in Kerry in a couple of hours. On horseback I hoped to be there in a couple of days, but would they allow me to board the ferry? It was a question that had been occupying me for some time. Mary Davoren had said, "If you can't get permission to lead her on then you've a good chance of catching a lift in a cattle truck. Lots of farmers go to Kerry to buy cattle so drive over with empty trucks." I would keep my options open. One thing I did know was that there was no alternative. The nearest bridge was in Limerick, an 80-mile journey on main roads. I planned a route to the ferry that avoided all busy roads, included a few *bohreens* (narrow lanes), and took me through the most interesting-looking countryside.

Mollie was drooping patiently by her telegraph pole. I'd felt very guilty about leaving her with nothing to eat but the neighbouring woman said she'd given her carrots and brown bread. "She's been as good as gold. Had lots of visitors." She looked as good as gold and so beautiful. I couldn't stop admiring her lovely clean sea-washed legs; they were usually assorted shades of brown. I felt one of my surges of love when I stroked her and fed her more carrots. I was so lucky.

Chapter 11

It just wasn't fair; whenever I tried to get off the busy roads I ran into trouble. Heading south from Lehinch I attempted to take a short cut along a newly surfaced track marked vaguely on the map in little dots. Perhaps it was just a glint in the cartographer's eye, since it meandered around, visiting farms, and lacked all sense of purpose, while our arrival caused great excitement with the local cattle. I kept thinking of the riddle 'Why did the cow slip? Because she saw the bull rush.' There were bulls rushing (or bullocks, anyway) and cows slipping all over the place in the mud. I didn't much like it when they rushed and slipped around me, especially when the road passed through their field. I closed the last gate behind me with relief. Then I heard a strange squeak and saw the most pathetic-looking donkey. Its hooves were so overgrown they curled up in the front like Turkish slippers, and a rope was tied so tightly around its throat that its bray was reduced to a noise like furniture being dragged over a polished floor. It was desperately lonely, and trotted along its side of the hedge with open mouth, squeak-braying at each breath. Mollie was a snob and ignored it completely, while I hastened to get away because it upset me so much.

The next hazard was a patch of peat bog. Two men were cutting the turf and stacking it into neat blocks. Beyond them was the road I was trying to

join. They walked over and were full of chat and helpful suggestions. "Can
the horse jump?" "Yes," I said, so they took down some wire at the top of the
bank bordering a stream. I had to slither down into the water and ask Mollie
to jump up the bank on the other side. She made a pointed demonstration
of the absurdity of the idea by resting her chin on the top of the bank. She
was right; it was much too high. The men, both of whom seemed to be called
Michael, had a consultation and agreed there was an easier place further
down. The bank was lower here, and after the trouble the two Michaels had
taken to dismantle the wire fence, I drove Mollie at it with determination
and she jumped up without hesitation. Mollie could always tell whether I
believed in what I was asking her to do, and more and more I was trusting
her with safety decisions. One of the Michaels escorted me to the road,
explaining it was time for his tea anyway. I rode along, chatting, although
I knew that it wasn't the road I wanted to be on. Instead of the five-mile
bohreen round a mountain that I'd planned, I ended up with an eight mile slog
along a main road. It was cold and cloudy and boring. I was angry and bored
and Mollie was stodgy and bored. I kicked her along the grass verge, cursing
cars and horses and Irish maps, and she looked for things to shy at. When I
trotted the saddlebags slipped, but I was too bad-tempered to try to balance
them. A silver strip of sea appeared on the horizon and this reminder that I
was heading west not south made me even crosser. Then it started to rain and
Mollie did her rain act – head down and sideways. "For Christ's sake, you're
a Connemara pony!" I shouted. "You can't tell me you're not used to rain."

Suddenly the sun burst out from behind a cloud and a rainbow sprang
up behind me. I found my turning off the main road; it was all so beautiful I
stopped being cross and gave Mollie a tea-break on the grass verge while I let
the usual feeling of tranquillity settle over me again. I watched the sea turn
from silver to blue, and a couple of hares frolicking in a close-cropped field.
The Irish hare is thought to be sub-species and they have a special reason to

be frolicsome: in times past it was believed that monks' souls entered into hares, so they were protected.

It was time to think about stopping for the night. As usual it took Mollie's decisiveness to end my procrastination. Each evening I rode along making up excuses: this house is too posh, that one's too poor, I'm sure there's no-one home here, or too many people home and looking at me there. Mollie knew the routine and when she reckoned it was time to stop for the night she'd snatch at grass on the roadside and try to turn down promising-looking driveways. Today it was quite late and she was sulking along having suggested various farms that I'd vetoed (the excuse – too early and why not enjoy the evening light) when we passed a pub standing by itself at a crossroad. 'Crosses of Annagh' was painted on its white walls. There was a family sound about it (my maiden name was Cross) and I waved at the people crowding the doorway as I went by. A pub would be full of farmers with fields and a Guinness would be good consolation for my unsatisfactory day. I turned back, tied Mollie to a gate and went in.

It was still early in the evening but a few men were quenching their thirst at the bar. Yes, several of them had a suitable field and yes, I'd be welcome to stay there. But first they had to finish their pint. And the next one. I fretted about Mollie who'd had a long day and meagre grazing last night. "Tell you what, try Sara across the road. She's got a garden that's all overgrown. You could put the pony there – and camp there. Sara wouldn't mind." And indeed she didn't. I led Mollie through the little garden gate and found a flattish place for the tent before turning her loose in the long grass and weeds with some apprehension. I didn't want her gazing through the window and embarrassing the occupants or manuring the garden path. I gave her a drink in a borrowed bucket and headed for the pub. The publican's wife showed me into a smaller side room, served me my Guinness, offered me sandwiches and introduced me to the sole occupant, a small, toothless man called Joe.

Now, as I've explained before, I'm not a pub person. Not even in England with friends. But it's part of the Irish scene and if I was to get to know the Real Ireland, slake my thirst, and have somewhere warm to go in the evening, I had to learn to be at ease in pubs. So there we were, just me and Joe, and we were both too shy to talk. We sipped our Guinness, and smiled, and kept our eyes lowered or gazed at the fire, and I wrote my diary. After that drink I went back to my tent, but returned to the bar when it was too dark to read. Two men, Michael and John, had joined Joe. John was a man of the world, having worked in Bournemouth and the Channel Islands, and he knew how to talk to ladies like me (I found out later he has a pub himself down the road). And because he was so friendly, jovial and funny, everyone began to talk and I felt properly part of the scene. I learned all about turf and silage, giggled over a lot of risqué jokes about women and mares (my feminist friends would be horrified) and heard what it's like to be an Irish construction worker in Bournemouth. Undiluted pleasure, apparently! John did most of the talking, with Joe and Michael listening and nodding. But Joe became much more forthcoming as the evening wore on. His bird eyes got brighter and brighter and he had a delightful toothless grin, especially when romantic suggestions were in the air. Joe was the sort of traditional Irishman that American anthropologists study. He'd suddenly come out with little snippets of folk-wisdom, like: 'Horses like Guinness. Did you know that? A man can drink, and come to a horse and it'll do anything for him. A horse likes a man with some drink inside him. A cow now, or a bull, it hates it.'

The evening ended with me stumbling off into the night to test Joe's theory on Mollie, and with a promise to visit John the next day at his pub in Mullagh, the next village.

It was Sunday. I arrived in Mullagh just before noon and found the high street full of tractors and other agricultural vehicles. I thought it must be a farm auction or something, but no, it was Mass. That's how you get to Mass if you're a farmer in these parts. With all the faithful in church the town was deserted, so I tied Mollie to a lamppost and went into John's pub. While I was drinking coffee and chatting, a crowd of men, dressed in their Sunday best, surged in talking about the horse outside. That made conversation easy – I just answered questions.

When I left the pub the street was full of little groups standing around gossiping, and a tight group of admirers were talking to Mollie. When I returned from my search for groceries I found that a man had untied Mollie and was giving pony rides to the local children.

I loved the straightforward Irish adherence to Catholicism. As I wrote later to Kate:

> People here are so open about their faith. None of our Church of England defensiveness about Christianity. It's part of life and sacred pictures are part of the home décor. I was in a delightful house last night which had the usual religious painting with its own broken red light giving eternal illumination. Jesus was staring down at his dripping sacred heart with a horrified 'What will Mum say?' expression.
>
> I think of Ireland as a Third World country, but in an entirely complimentary, happy way. If I'd come here from England without seeing Peru, etc first, the culture shock would have been much greater. It's the friendliness and hospitality, the lack of any consciousness of time or efficiency, and the grumblings at the government which seem so familiar. There are also the negative aspects. There's real poverty – the farmer I stayed with last night has no car yet lives miles from the nearest town and there's no bus service – rubbish is dumped in beauty spots and dead cars litter the countryside. They lie peacefully in their green graveyards like so many dozing cows; they're up-turned in hedges, nestling in bracken, dumped in fields and nose-dived in

ditches. Many old cars refuse to die, however. The MOT test seems to be just a formality, with no relationship to actual road-worthiness, so cars have no bumpers, or have holes in the floor, as in Africa.

And talking of holes, the Irish must have the worst teeth in the world. One frequently finds young people in their twenties with a full set of false teeth and I'm no longer surprised to be greeted with a gummy smile from women my own age. Teeth-pulling seems to be part of the Irish way of life. I thought I was getting a clue last night when the subject of high dental fees came up. 'What do they charge?' I asked.

'Jesus God, it's seven punts an extraction!'

'How about fillings?'

'Oh, I don't think he does those.'

A landowner told me about his farmhand who complained, 'I'm getting neither ease nor pleasure from my teeth. And when I went to the dentist to have them drew, he told me to come back in six weeks when the stumps was well rotted.'

Our amble south from Mullagh was lovely. No spectacular scenery but sunny weather with no wind – the first day I'd been able just to wear a T-shirt – and I could clip-clop along, thinking my thoughts, greeting the occasional passer-by (cars often stopped for the drivers to have a chat) and looking at flowers and butterflies. The hedgerows looked and smelled like my childhood. The grass and the flowers aren't cut back and I remembered the names I learned as a child: speedwell, potentilla tormentilla, scarlet pimpernel – and orange-tip butterflies. There were geese and cows in the fields instead of sheep, and a warm feeling of summer. I say I was thinking my own thoughts but usually they were non-thoughts. I'd anticipated that on a trip like this I'd work out the Meaning of Life or My Place in the Universe, but instead words arranged themselves in my subconscious to the rhythm of Mollie's hoof beats.

One day it was relentlessly 'What'll we do with the butter mountain?', and I generally found myself singing either 'Molly Malone' or 'It's a long way to Tipperary' – which I expected to reach in a month or so.

I did reflect on God from time to time. As an agnostic I have no faith but a curiosity about things spiritual. That day of warm sunshine and flowers, and Mollie's pricked grey ears in front of me, a thought pinged into my mind: 'God is love'. Well of course we've all heard that expression *ad nauseam*, and because it's so familiar I'd never thought what it meant. But here I reflected on love in all its facets, and how it sets us above animals. That day I was travelling in a pool of love, love for the sun, the flowers, the colours – and above all, for Mollie. And I realised there was no evolutionary reason to feel that way.

My warm, happy feelings continued into the evening. We were walking down a very narrow lane when a man herding cows stopped me to have a chat. Tom had dark curly hair, well-patched trousers, and was so friendly and interested that we talked for quite a while until Mum appeared in her bedroom slippers to find out what was going on. Although it was only 6 o'clock I asked if I could stay in one of their fields. They were delighted and removed some calves from the paddock near the house, and then of course I was invited in for tea. After I got the tent set up I asked to use the loo. "Ye'll find a place!" they both said laughing. The house was the sort that's described in books as 'simply furnished but neat as two pins'. There were three rooms, so the kitchen/sitting room was also a storeroom, with bags of potatoes and farm implements stacked by the walls. The only furniture was a table, two or three hardback chairs and a settee. The floor was cement and tea water boiled on an ancient turf-burning stove. Apart from a religious painting and a calendar there was a 1940s wireless that didn't work and an even earlier clock with a loud tick. We spent such an agreeable evening together, drinking tea and eating brown bread. Mum sat snapping sticks for kindling while we discussed hospital care ("Oh God, I thought my heart would stop there and then"), the evils of television ("Oh Lord I wouldn't have one in the house!") to farming, marriage and whether politicians should tell the truth.

I also discussed my current preoccupation – whether I would be allowed to take Mollie onto the ferry across the River Shannon. "Ah, ye'll have no problem, just chat to them first," was the consensus here. I'd read about an earlier traveller who had reached the Shannon and been unable to get across. O'Sullivan Beare, an Irish chieftain, was impeded by the river when fleeing from the English in 1602. His men were starving and there were no boats, so he neatly solved both problems by killing his horses, eating their meat and using the hides to make curraghs.

I arrived early at the pier before there was much traffic, tied Mollie to a lamppost, and when the first ferry arrived I tripped nimbly up the gangplank to talk to the husky ferryman. "Absolutely not!"

"But. . . but there's a notice there saying 'Livestock carried at your own risk'. Well, I'll take the risk!"

"They have to be in a cattle truck."

"I'll buy you a glass of Guinness at the pub!"

"Listen, I said no and I meant no. If my boss found out we'd all lose our jobs."

He turned away and started directing the waiting cars.

I took off Mollie's saddlebags, attached the long lead rope to her head collar and sat down to wait for an empty horsebox or cattle truck to arrive. Now I'm used to hitchhiking – indeed, I've hitchhiked all my adult life – but this was the first time I'd tried hitchhiking with a horse, and it wasn't easy. Two more ferries came and went, and around noon I made a decision. I tied Mollie to the lamppost again, heaped the luggage beside her and went back to talk to a just-back-from-living-in-Canada publican who I'd chatted with on my way down to the ferry, when the urge for a loo hit me. His name was Pierce and he owned the pub that served beer to passengers waiting for the ferry (this charming place has now been replaced by a pseudo castle selling coffee and souvenirs). The pub was crowded and I hated asking him to pause from pulling pints to listen to my problem, feeling anything but reassured when he said he'd see what he could do. He was clearly too busy to do anything; I'd hoped that he would just point out a horsebox owner in the pub. I tried to take matters into my own hands and asked some of the more accessible-looking men nearby if they were local. They all said no, winked at their friends and burst out laughing, so I sat in a corner and drank Guinness, ate crisps and worried about Mollie and my gear abandoned by the river. I went out to check on them both, gave Mollie a consolation carrot, and returned to the pub for a sandwich and gloomy contemplation. The 1-o'clock ferry came in, the drinkers drained their glasses and left, and suddenly the pub was almost empty. I asked the barmaid where Pierce was and she said he'd gone out. My gloom deepened. Why should I think that a busy publican would bother to help a complete stranger?

Then I looked out of the window. Outside was what looked like a large orange-crate on wheels attached to a rather smart red car. Pierce got out of the car, walked into the pub and said, "Ready?" I was almost speechless. Here was an actual horsebox – of sorts – and despite all my fretting, less than an hour had passed since I'd arrived with my problem. Pierce apologised for the delay – apologised! – and said it was his cousin's trailer but they'd had difficulty finding a car to tow it so Pierce would use his own and drive across. "But what about your customers?" I spluttered. He shrugged and looked at his watch. "We've just got time to catch the 2-o'clock ferry." So I raced ahead, found Mollie and the gear still intact, led her up to the ramp of the orange crate, heaved the luggage into the back of the car, and got into the passenger seat with Pierce's young son for the short drive onto the ferry.

"Only in Ireland!" I heard an American tourist say as I fed carrots to Mollie during the crossing, then we drove down the ramp into Co Kerry, quickly unloaded Mollie and my gear, Pierce turned around and joined the queue of cars waiting to board for the return journey to Co Clare.

Chapter 12

At last I was in Kerry. I'd looked forward to my arrival for some time. After all, it's the county that attracts the most tourists because of its mountain scenery, and despite my teenage misery-memories of squelching through bogs in the rain, I also remembered the wild rocky hills and deep valleys of the Dingle Peninsula where we had stayed. I could see the mountains of Slieve Mish across the flatness of northern Kerry.

After the ferry crossing I headed for Ballybunion (at the request of my right foot) along a gentle road running between large fields. It felt quite different from Co Clare. More prosperous somehow, with larger farms, more cattle, no sheep. But the Real Ireland was never far away and we met our first ever pony and cart – much to Mollie's delight, and mine, since she quickened her pace to catch up. "That's a grand pony!" said the tinker. "How old?" But he was already out of the cart and looking in her mouth. No, I said firmly, I really didn't want to swap her for his little chestnut gelding.

Since much of that day had been spent trying to get across the Shannon, I'd planned to ride well into the evening but Mollie had other ideas. She slowed down hopefully at every driveway, while I told her it was much too early to stop. I gave in when we passed a really beautiful farm; its long drive was bordered by trees shading large fields of very green grass, and I rode up to the farmhouse under the speculative gaze of two boys. Although I was getting a little braver about asking farmers for hospitality I still hated that initial approach, and sat stiffly in the saddle until they were within earshot.

Mollie ended up in the best field of the trip, with the cows safely in an adjacent field and a water trough should she deign to drink. It was a dairy farm and Mum had told me to come to the house for milk, but first I sat outside the tent and wrote up my diary, pausing at intervals to watch Mollie grazing. Considering the amount of exercise she was getting she looked remarkably fat. Oh gosh, I wouldn't be surprised if Willie had absentmindedly let a stallion into the field. I was an accomplished worrier, and every day I checked her obsessively for sores or lameness. While preparing for the trip I had bought a little book about horse problems, and read in horror about poll evil, spavins, windgalls, laminitis, and navicular disease. With four legs to go wrong, there was plenty to worry about, yet I had to admit that Mollie was in perfect physical shape. She looked lovely, and I was so proud of her.

Time for supper. I went in for a bucket of water for my morning ablutions and a bottle of milk and was offered a chair and *Dynasty*, along with tea with masses of brown bread and biscuits.

I was woken the next morning by rooks cawing in the trees above the tent, had my usual muesli and coffee (with fresh milk), then hearing heavy breathing poked my head out of the tent to find Mollie a few yards away being investigated by a herd of white Charolais bullocks which had just been let into the field. When they saw me they stampeded but Mollie didn't give a damn, being intent on catching up with her eating before it was time to go. She knew the day's routine so well now. I could spy on her through the tent flaps when I first unzipped the door from the warmth of my sleeping bag, and see her dozing in the morning sun. She generally stayed near the tent during the night, and would watch my movements as I got dressed and heated water on the little stove for coffee. Then she would have her own breakfast, determined to eat as much as possible before hitting the road. She didn't have to worry today. Sheila beckoned me from the house and asked if I'd like a cup of tea. On the kitchen table was not only tea but sausages, bread and butter and marmalade. While I ate (I'm never one to be put off a meal because I've just eaten one) Sheila talked.

I learned that she was one of 14 children. "When I was a child there was no free secondary education in Ireland. My parents sent me to America to live with a childless aunt and uncle. I was so miserable! I was only 14 and I missed all my brothers and sisters. Aunty wasn't used to children and everything seemed so strange at first. But I settled down, went to college, and got a good job in New York. But we Irish always come home, you know. I never intended to stay there. I came back and married and here we are." I remarked what a beautiful farm it was, how its well-fenced green fields and white-washed buildings had caught my eye from the road. "But you should see it in the winter! Mud everywhere. It's terrible then." The conversation turned to the North. "You won't find many people who want a united Ireland. In many ways the Catholics across the border are better off than we are. Child allowance, for instance. They get more family allowance in one week up there than we get here in a month!"

Ballybunion was described in my guidebook as 'a popular holiday resort on a dramatic coastline of cave-riddled cliffs on the shores of a bay warmed by the Gulf Stream. Dividing the golden strand in front of the town is a promontory with the remains of late 16th-century Ballybunion Castle, a Fitzmaurice stronghold. . . and a golf course considered to be one of the best in the world.' We arrived around noon and found a path leading past some caravans to the beach. It was all as described, caves carved into the cliffs by the pounding surf, a long stretch of the deserted golden beach, and some golfers high on the cliff top who didn't even look up as I galloped by.

I pulled up by some dunes and decided this would be a good place for lunch. I could get out of the wind and there was a little grass for Mollie.

These days I didn't tether her; I took her bit out and let her wander around, grazing. And that day I didn't even bother to zip up the saddlebag after pulling out my plastic bag containing Sheila's brown bread and butter, and a pot of marmite. I sat on the sand in the sun, ate some of my lunch, read a little Yeats and looked for Ballyduff on my map.

I was now preoccupied with Mollie's shoes, having seen how thin they were when I picked out her hooves that morning. A front shoe was cracked in half and slightly loose. I had to find a blacksmith soon and had been told I might find one in Ballyduff, about five miles away. Suddenly there was a commotion behind me.

Mollie had taken off at a gallop. She laboured up a sand dune, veered round at the top, slid down and continued up and down the dunes in circles, skidding in the soft sand, while bits and pieces flew out of the open saddlebag. I stared at her open-mouthed. It wasn't high spirits (very unlikely with phlegmatic Mollie), I could see that she was really scared. It took a few moments for me to realise what had happened. Out of the corner of her eye she had caught sight of a white plastic bag protruding from the unzipped saddlebag. Mollie had always had something of a phobia about plastic bags and had tried to escape this menace but it continued to pursue her, threatening her left flank, whatever evasive action she took. "Whoa Mollie, it's alright!" She galloped past me but on her next circuit I managed to grab her rope. She was still very frightened, breathing hard with dilated nostrils and wide eyes. The breeze fluttered the plastic, still sticking out of the saddlebag, and she tried to take off again, dragging me with her. I managed to hold on and block her view of the offending piece of plastic while I calmed her down and zipped up the bag.

This behaviour came as a complete surprise. It wasn't the first time I'd left the saddlebag open and Mollie was always totally placid while I rummaged around there. Indeed it had always impressed me that she was willing to stand quietly while I heaved the bags onto her back, often missing the first time (they hadn't got any lighter) and banging her flanks as I struggled. In an instant this had all changed. It was a long time before Mollie's breathing returned to normal, and I repacked my picnic stuff in slow motion, talking to her quietly as I did so.

I had hoped to ford the River Cashen at the end of the beach but the tide was in and I didn't want to subject Mollie to any more unpleasantness. Following a track along the river I passed some salmon fishermen, bright in their yellow oilskins, hauling in their nets. No luck today, they told me. At Ballyduff's general store I bought my lunch, including an apple for Mollie, and some more packets of soup. I always tried to carry enough food for one night of wild camping since I never knew where I would end up. To my great relief, the shopkeeper knew where the blacksmith lived, though it was three miles away. "Just keep straight along that road. You can't miss it."

"Oh dear no, I don't shoe horses any more," said Michael. "I stopped seven years ago on account of my thumb, see." He showed me the scar. "No strength in my left hand. I'd do you the favour, mind, but you'd have to bring your own shoes. You can get them in Lerrig, and there's a farrier nearby who can nail them on. Just a minute, I'll measure her hooves for you... size 5½ you'll need, and don't forget to buy 26 nails."

My route was now dictated by my quest for a blacksmith, and my comfort by Mollie's new phobia. I stopped for the night near Causeway, en route to Lerrig, camping in a garden, and next morning covered the saddlebags with plastic to protect them from the rain. But Mollie was having none of it. She wouldn't let me come near her. I had to remove the plastic and just hope the rain would hold off; which it did, despite slabs of slate-grey cloud looking near enough to touch.

Lerrig was nothing more than a shop, but what a wonderful shop! It was multi-roomed and sold everything: carrots and apples, cabbages and hay, sweaters and stockings, hardware and horseshoes. With Mollie so jumpy I was nervous about leaving her, and before tying her up I checked the area for lurking plastic bags.

'I want a set of horse shoes, size 5½ please. Oh, and 26 nails.'

"I'll give you two extra, just in case," said the very friendly shopkeeper. "A farrier? There's one not far from here." He came out to admire Mollie and show me the way. "If you go a mile along that road you'll see the smithy on the right. He still does horses."

As well as shoes I bought a tether chain. More weight to carry but it eliminated the danger of the rope getting round Mollie's leg. If I needed to tether her again during the day I didn't want a repeat of the Cliffs of Moher scene. As I'd learned with Johnny so many years ago, the weight of a chain keeps it on the ground and under hoof. Much safer.

The new shoes and chain weighed down the saddlebag causing it to slip to one side. I felt that lop-sided luggage must be uncomfortable for Mollie and was forever pulling it back into position, only to watch it slowly slide down again. It wasn't worth re-balancing the bags when I was so near the blacksmith. After two miles I knocked at a door to ask directions from an admiring woman in rollers. The forge was only a few more doors down. "I hope he's there." So did I, but he wasn't. At least I could get no reply when I hammered on the door. Two apologetic black mongrels cringed in the garden, their wagging tails clamped between their legs. My knocks roused a neighbour from the caravan next door who came to help. He prowled around the house trying doors and said the smith was probably asleep. "He's fond of the. . ." And he raised an imaginary drink to his mouth.

I sulked back to the horseshoe shop, hauling the slipping bags up and cursing Mollie for needing footwear. I remembered a dream I'd had years ago about riding a pony to the blacksmith. "I'm taking him to get new shoes," I called out to a friend. Whereupon the pony turned around and said "But I don't want shoes, I want slippers!"

The shop manager was sympathetic and told me I'd certainly get the shoes done in Tralee. "There's a blacksmith in Station Road, right in the centre of town. Ask for Paddy." I'd hoped to avoid Tralee. Despite the romantic association with the 'Rose of Tralee' I'd been warned that "it's no more than a dirty ugly old town!" Irish songs are about people, not places. The 'Rose of Tralee' isn't about Tralee, it's about Mary, a kitchen maid who was 'lovely and fair as the rose in the summer' and who died of a broken heart when her lover, the son of her employer, was sent away by his irate mother and married someone else. It was he (William Mulchinock) who wrote the song at her graveside. (Or so they say. He must have been a fast worker.)

At least I now had a new song in my head and you can't sing and remain in a bad mood. Mollie, with no song in her head, kept hers and crept along thinking about plastic bags. The sun peered out from behind black clouds as I approached Ardfert. If I couldn't get a blacksmith, at least I could get history. Ardfert, with its cathedral and ruined friary, is one of the main tourist sights in flat and boring northwest Kerry. Having just ridden on to a new map, rich in promise of lakes and high mountains, I was impatient to reach Dingle.

I enjoyed the Ardfert ruins, despite my nervousness over leaving Mollie tethered to a gate covered with warning notices about fierce greyhounds. I'd asked permission and a woman had said darkly, "She'll be alright as long as the dogs don't see her." They didn't. The monastery was founded in the 6th century by St Brendan whom I'd adopted as my patron saint. He was a navigator, not a horseman, but maybe he did discover America and he certainly got around his own country and the outlying islands. There are

St Brendan mementos everywhere, mostly in the scenic parts of Kerry. The saint received his education at Ardfert and became the best-selling writer of his times. The account of his voyages was translated into English, Welsh, Gaelic, Breton, Saxon, Flemish, Latin and French – pretty good going before the invention of the printing press. He had lots of adventures, including encountering a crystal mountain (an iceberg, maybe?) and once celebrating Easter Mass and lighting a fire on a domed island which turned out to be an indignant whale!

The roofless and glassless cathedral up the road reminded me of Tintern Abbey and other such British ruins. A symbol of the power of the Church in medieval times, it had a fine Romanesque doorway, splendid east windows, and some fancy crenulations.

The rain held off as I urged Mollie down the busy main road towards Tralee and the blacksmith – 10 miles away. As I approached the town a strong wind blew up and with the wind came flying plastic bags. It was a horrible ride, ugly and dangerous with Mollie frequently shying into the road into the path of the rush-hour traffic. I was soon lost in a complex of housing and industrial estates. No-one had heard of a Tralee blacksmith, and as I followed their vague directions to Station Road my heart sank as I realised it was indeed bang in the centre of town; I couldn't imagine that he would shoe horses in that location. If only these people had telephones! Station Road, when I finally got there, was narrow and jammed with cars but I could see blue flashes coming from a large open building that I rightly guessed to be the forge. I got off and waited for Paddy to come out to me, Mollie pulling back in fright at the sight and sound of the welding. "Haven't done horses for 20 years," he said, without a smile. "Whoever told you to come here?" I felt near to tears. "I reckon you won't find anyone in Dingle either. No call for it now, see!"

"But they told me in Clare that there would be plenty of farriers in Kerry."

"Did they now."

While we were talking, an elegantly dressed woman with what I guessed to be a German accent came up to marvel at Mollie and our achievements. "How far do you go each day?"

"About 20 miles, on average."

"Goodness, that's very impressive."

"No, it isn't," broke in Paddy the non-farrier. "In days back you'd take a pony 40 or 50 miles in a trap."

"But isn't it easier for a harness pony? Once it gets going there must be very little work involved. Poor Mollie's got to carry me and my luggage. Anyway, I couldn't do more than 20 miles or so. My bottom and knees get sore." I was feeling thoroughly fed up and not inclined to stand there chatting, holding a hungry pony. The woman spoke again.

"Do you need somewhere to spend the night?"

"Do I ever!"

"I run an independent hostel and we used to have our own pony so there's a field. It's only 20 minutes from here." I felt instantly cheered. At least I could have a dry night (the rain was not going to hold off forever) and make a few phone calls. There was a pony trekking centre near Tralee and they would certainly know of a blacksmith who still did horses.

The Dromtacker Hostel was a long 20 minutes away and the field a bit sparse. I led Mollie past a caravan to a grassy glade full of rusting machinery and washing. As I walked away I found her following me with pricked ears and a 'you can't mean *here*?' expression on her face. She'd been spoiled by last night's luxury. I pulled her tether rope across the opening, and added further deterrents to escape while the rain came down in torrents. I was glad to be inside, with the cheerful chatter of the hostellers and the shrieks of a horde of children, presumably belonging to the warden.

It was still raining hard the next morning, but at least there was a public phone at the hostel so I was able to phone William O'Connor.

His pony trekking stable, El Rancho, was well known and I couldn't waste
any more time looking for blacksmiths. He would advise me. I also wanted
to learn about off-road routes through those tempting-looking mountains
on the Dingle peninsula. If anyone knew about them, William would. Mrs
O'Connor answered the phone. "I'm afraid my husband's away on a trek, but
do come here for coffee and I'll see what I can do to help."

I found Ballyard on the map, just south of Tralee, and while waiting
for the skies to brighten, I carefully encased the saddlebags in black, non-
flapping plastic. I was determined to keep my kit dry. Earlier, Mollie had
come up to me with a little whinny, clearly enthusiastic about the day ahead
and the possibility of better grazing. I felt confident that her bag phobia
would not be triggered by my inoffensive waterproofing, but nevertheless
enlisted one of the other hostellers to help load her up.

I tied her to a tree, spoke soothing words and we approached with the
saddlebags. She pulled back and the branch snapped. More soothing words,
a thicker rope and a stouter tree. Again we approached, one holding each
side of the saddlebags so that we could lay it gently on her back. She pulled
back with all her strength – I could see the muscles in her shoulder and neck
bulge with the effort – and something gave. From my position behind her I
couldn't see her head but could hear a dreadful noise like a steam train leaving
the station. Mollie's beautiful Peruvian head collar, designed to withstand
recalcitrant Andean mules, had broken and the noseband was tight round
her nostrils, suffocating her. Thank God I had her tied with a slip knot. I'd
thought the head collar such a good design with the noseband tightening
when the rope was pulled – I never dreamed that it could be broken. Indeed,
only a few days earlier someone was telling me about horses breaking head
collars and I said smugly "not my head collar". The person looked at me
scornfully and said, "A horse can break anything!" Since the head collar was
also the bridle I was in trouble, though I managed an improvised repair.

Then of course I had to take off all that plastic that I'd so laboriously wrapped round the bags. Finally we were able to lift them onto Mollie's back, although it took ages. She was in a real state. Then all the children wanted pony rides which normally I wouldn't mind but it seemed foolhardy this morning. There was such a wailing when I said no, so I gave in, and although she was patient with them my heart was in my mouth.

It had taken an hour to get under way. Now the offending plastic was gone, Mollie was quiet enough, but it was still a horrid ride to Ballyard with lots of traffic and lots of plastic and I knew that Mollie considered the latter posed the greatest danger.

El Rancho was a beautiful place, and over coffee Anne O'Connor and I pored over William's brochures so I could see the routes he took with his pony-trekking clients around and across the peninsula. She didn't know the details, however; I would have to phone her husband for more information in one of his overnight places. She gave me the number. But she did know, definitely, that there was a farrier in Castlemaine, "over the mountains" by the name of O'Shea. And he did still shoe horses? For sure.

The road over the mountains was perfect, with a line of grass running down the centre and verges to provide a non-slip surface. Bluebells were still hanging on in sheltered glades under the beech trees, and a river tumbled down from the Slieve Mish Mountains to my right. As we climbed towards the highest point, the trees disappeared and I was surrounded by bare peaks and rain-washed rocks, with not a house in sight. Such a contrast to north Kerry and horrible Tralee. The sun came out when I reached the top of the hill, and I could see Macgillycuddy's Reeks to the south, where I had climbed Carrauntoohil, Ireland's highest mountain, on that family holiday all those years ago.

Only one car passed and the driver stopped to talk. He was flatteringly impressed at what I was doing and thought it was all a marvellous idea.

"What'll you do with the pony when you finish the ride?"

"Oh, I'll find a way of taking her back to England. I couldn't possibly sell her now!"

What? I really had to get a grip on myself, of all impractical ideas this took the biscuit.

It was 7 o'clock when I reached Castlemaine so my plan was to locate the blacksmith and make an appointment for Mollie to be shod the next day. I found what I thought was the forge and asked a youth sitting on a tractor in the yard if this was the blacksmith's house. He jumped down and hid behind the vehicle. Taken aback, I asked the two eyes peeping behind the wheel, "Excuse me, sorry to frighten you, is this the blacksmith's?" Once I got closer I realised that the boy had Down's Syndrome. Then mum came out, saw me, and said, "Well, isn't this marvellous!" And marvellous it was for the next 15 hours. I have never been with a family where love was so evident, love turned both inwards to the family and out to anyone fortunate enough to come into their sphere. When Beth said of the silent boy, "Joe-Joe's our treasure," I knew this was the truth. There were four children and a bachelor uncle who got lonely living up the road by himself so now lived with the family, and Dinny the blacksmith who lost an eye on the job. I met the charming and mature daughter, but lost my heart to 12-year-old Anthony who was so polite and interested and just knew by instinct everything that needed doing.

Dinny had a quick look at Mollie's feet and, with relief, I handed over the shoes and nails which had been weighing down my saddlebag. "I'll do her first thing in the morning," he said.

There was no question of me finding accommodation elsewhere in Castlemaine. Mollie was tethered on some waste ground full of the usual rusting machinery, but with a good supply of grass and within snorting distance of the tent, and I was invited in for tea and biscuits in front of a cosy turf fire. I stayed chatting all evening, enveloped in the warmth of the family, all the stresses of the last few days disappearing.

When eventually my protestations that I really must go to bed were accepted, I was escorted to my tent by Anthony, clutching a hot water bottle in one hand and a mug of Bournevita in the other. I slept like a log and woke guiltily at 8.30 to the sound of metal hitting metal and a few minutes later Anthony was outside saying, "I'll take Mollie to the forge now. Mum has breakfast ready for you." On the kitchen table was a plate heaped with mushrooms, tomatoes, sausage, egg and bacon, and in case I was still hungry there was brown bread, toast and marmalade. By the time I'd staggered out to see how the shoeing was going, it was almost finished. Mollie's forefoot was resting on the tripod while Dinny filed away the overgrown hoof. The red-hot shoes had been burned into position so were unlikely to loosen during my next 400 miles. That's how long the previous set had lasted. I had paid IR£25 for those so had been to the bank in Tralee in preparation for this major expense. "How much do I owe you?" I asked.

"Six punts."

"Six punts! Are you sure?"

"Well I usually charge eight but. . ."

I paid eight. The next customer arrived, a jaunty brown pony pulling a cart, so I took a photo, said an almost tearful goodbye and set off towards Dingle.

Chapter 13

Mollie stepped out in her new shoes like a child in new wellingtons. For days I'd had her balancing along narrow grass verges to save her feet, but now she could trot briskly along the roads. And I was in the real Kerry at last! The showers couldn't dampen my euphoria; besides, they provided rainbows over Castlemaine Harbour. Beyond the silver bay were rows of mountains in different shades of grey against a rain-filled sky. It was the first of June. There were still bluebells beside the road and occasional primroses, but the fields were now full of yellow flag. Silly to hurry; I'd give Mollie a lunch break by the sea and have some of Beth's brown bread and the yoghurt I'd bought in the town.

After packing away my lunch I propped my elbows on the saddle and studied the map. I'd discussed possible off-road routes with William on the phone but was still undecided on where to go next. I considered retracing my steps towards Tralee to intercept his group as they returned to the stables. His knowledge of the peninsula would be such a help, and he could show me on the map the route he took between the high mountains above Lough Anascaul. Amid such beautiful scenery I longed to get away from roads and cars. However, my late start and the bad weather discouraged me – I'd have to hurry to meet the group and what was the point of going high if clouds hid the view? Probably I should just push on to the town of Dingle – the map showed all sorts of tempting back-roads. But tomorrow would be the start of the Whit Weekend and the town would be packed with holiday-makers. . . I'd continue west and decide tomorrow.

At Inch, 12 miles from Castlemaine, a dune-bordered finger of land projects into the sea. Between the dunes and the waves were three miles of hard sand – perfect for a gallop. No one else was around as we thudded through the surf and frolicked in the dunes. I felt a bit like a child playing on her own. Like hard times, fun times are best shared. Perhaps with a companion I would have gone right to Inch Point but I was content to stop after a couple of miles and walk Mollie quietly back. I needed to catch my breath, not she. She was superbly fit now after her regular 15 to 20 slow miles a day. I felt that we could travel forever.

If the scenery had been beautiful before Inch, it was stunning now. The road followed high indented cliffs flecked with cormorants and gulls. Blocks of white rain obscured parts of the mountains on the other side of the bay while the sun played on selected peaks bringing a blobby rainbow. I felt tears pricking my eyes. How perfect to ride past such beauty at two or three miles an hour, able to see every shifting pattern of light over the breaking surf. Normally I wouldn't sit and stare at a view for an hour – I'm too impatient – but on Mollie I could gaze all day while the scenery slowly changed. What could be better?

As I approached Anascaul the sun edged the clouds with silver and lit green fields beneath the brown dour-faced mountains. It seemed the loveliest town in Ireland. I would find a bed and breakfast place and celebrate Mollie's shoes and the Real Kerry. On the outskirts of town I saw a sign 'Evening Meals'. Why not have a binge? An Englishman emerged from the garden and said sorry, his wife was away and it was she who did the cooking. But he suggested a B&B and a pony-owning girl who could probably put Mollie up for the night. A little further on I was greeted by another Englishman. "Do you know about the old road over the mountains? It's lovely! Goes to Castle Gregory."

"Could I make it on horseback?"

"Should do. After all, it used to be a road. See you in the pub tonight!"

While looking for the pony owner I passed the South Pole Inn which seemed a particularly inappropriate name in verdant Anascaul. I learned later that it was built and named by the Antarctic explorer, Tom Crean. He was in the search party that found the bodies of Captain Scott and his companions. I wondered how often someone leaves that pub saying, "I am just going outside and may be some time."

There was scant information about Crean in Anascaul in 1984, but now there's a statue and a thriving Tom Crean Society in the town, with lectures, events and excursions commemorating this modest man. It is said that when he retired to Anascaul he 'put all of his medals away and never again spoke about his experiences in the Antarctic' although this is contradicted by the story that when his wife reprimanded him for cooking up eggs and bacon on a meatless Friday he responded: "If you had been where I have been some Fridays I would have eaten a slice off your arse." Crean had plenty to boast about. He spent more time in Antarctica than either Scott or Shackleton – and outlived them both. Two acts of extreme heroism stand out: having accompanied Captain Scott to within 180 miles of the South Pole he was sent back with two companions while the remaining team of five completed their ill-fated journey to the Pole. He wept with disappointment at not being chosen. When one man, Evans, fell sick on the return trek, Crean volunteered to walk alone to the supply hut to get help. Already weakened by the arduous 1,500-mile trek – pulling a sledge – that he'd just accomplished, and with only some chocolate and three biscuits to sustain him, he walked the 35 miles in 18 hours. His action saved the lives of the two men, and he was awarded the Albert Medal from King George V. Two years later he was on Shackleton's *Endeavour* when it was crushed by the ice in Antarctica. Crean guided one of the lifeboats to Elephant Island and then made the 800-mile journey by small boat to South Georgia. Ironically the only time he reached the South Pole was when he came home to his pub.

∩ ∩ ∩

Cathy was delighted to give Mollie her field for the night – her pony was elsewhere – and to have a short ride. She got off enviously, explaining that her pony was spoiled and very lazy. Mollie was lucky, after two nights of indifferent grazing in back yards she had a large field of short nutritious grass. I too was lucky. The Four Winds B&B just up the road had a vacancy. I didn't go to the pub; I can't even remember if I had an evening meal. I do remember luxuriating in a hot bath, chuckling with delight at the sight of a bed, and feeling guilty about my grubby, greasy, white-hairy saddlebags in such a lovely clean room. I washed some clothes and reorganised my luggage, looking out my Swiss Army knife and sewing kit so that I could repair the head collar. I like mending; it took an hour, but I was proud of the result. It would break if subjected to a hard pull, but perhaps that was no bad thing. Then I got out the maps and the brochures given to me by Anne O'Connor, and tried to work out the route of that old road over the mountains, which was only partially shown on my inadequate map. It was clear up to Lough Anascaul, and I could see its general direction over the col between two mountains and down to the broad river valley leading to Castle Gregory. William took his trekking groups along this route and had told me on the phone that the 'Valley of the Cows' was beautiful – but that I'd never find my way in from the north. But I was now on the south side and felt sure that this track would be easy enough to follow. I'd been on tarred roads long enough, and had sufficient confidence now to do a little exploring. Besides, these mountains were the stuff of legends. Many, many years ago, around the time of Christ, there lived a small fierce Irishman called Cuchulainn. This Cuchulainn was apparently irresistible to women, which got him into all sorts of scraps. Near Anascaul he nearly met his match. His adversary was a giant, the woman who loved him was Scal Ni Mhurnain, and the weapons were boulders. The two warriors exchanged missiles for a week before Cuchulainn was hit. Scal, hearing his cry and thinking him dead, drowned herself in the lake at the foot of the mountains, hence An Scal.

Next morning I told my hosts of my plans. Kathleen immediately said, "Oh no, that's much too dangerous, you should go by the main road." I smiled patiently and explained that the whole point of riding a pony was to get off the roads and see the scenery denied to car drivers. Her husband, PJ, joined in. "There are places where there's a sheer drop. Walkers, have been killed there." I was not deterred. "Well I'm pretty experienced in mountains now, and I have a map and compass. If I come to cliffs I'll lead the pony. If one of us is going over, it had better be her." He looked out of the window. "At least the weather's improving. But the green road doesn't go all the way, you know. There's a cross-country stretch, I think you have to go northwest." Looking at the map and William's brochure, I agreed with him.

Mollie threw up her head when I came to the gate and started to walk towards me, her nostrils fluttering with her now familiar whicker. I told her we were going to have a special adventure today, gave her a thorough grooming and picked out her feet, admiring her new shoes, and took my final directions from Kathleen and PJ for the lane up to the lake. By the time we reached Lough Anascaul, rain clouds were whisking over the brown mountains and the lake shone grey in the dull light. A few cars were parked on the tarmac, their owners staring fixedly at the lake through carefully closed windows.

The enticing green road zigzagged up the hill between waterfalls and boulders left from Cuchlain's fight. Mollie, feeling grass beneath her feet instead of hard road, walked eagerly, head up, ears pricked. "This is what we came for, isn't it, Mollie girl?" I commented. My heart soared, although the old road was not without obstacles. Two stone walls blocked the track. The first was well built, and the most movable stones were to the right of an old stone pillar which presumably once supported a gate. The gap I made was narrow and when I led Mollie through, her saddlebag caught on the pillar. She surged forward nervously, ripping the canvas. I was annoyed with myself, having no suitable material with which to patch it and cursed my laziness for not making a wider gap. The next wall was easier, and soon we crossed a bridge over the tumbling river; the views, even in this dull weather, became dramatic. Grey slabs of rock beetled over the steep, boulder-strewn slopes, cut by cascading waterfalls, while the level ground was green with tussock grass and fluffy clumps of bog cotton. Behind me, and below, was the silvery lake and fading into the distance the green fields of Anascaul and blue-grey distant mountains. The path was clear and easy to follow, sometimes marshy, but not boggy, and we were soon near the col that marked the top of the Anascaul valley. In front of me was a broad, flattish area. I had been keeping an eye on the hoof-prints which periodically showed me I was not the first rider up the track that week, but was distracted by the fine views and it took a while for me to realise the prints had disappeared. Then the track ended.

The last section had been little more than a marsh between banks. Now the guiding banks had gone and I could see nothing but coarse clumps of grass separated by black muddy rivulets. Suddenly Mollie was floundering in bog. Her hind quarters went in above the hocks, she struggled free then sank again, this time up to her belly. Here she stayed, breathing heavily, head outstretched, chin resting on the ground. I had jumped off as she went down, and tried to undo the saddlebags, but my hands were shaking too much. From watching others on Willie's trek I knew Mollie would try again once she regained her breath. She did, but still to no avail. Desperately, I fumbled

again to relieve her of the weight of the saddlebags, but couldn't reach the straps. I tugged hard on the lead rope and urged her to try again. Summoning all her strength she made a supreme effort, reaching up with her forelegs, her head thrust forward for balance and back legs thrashing until she succeeded in freeing herself. She stood panting on firm ground, her legs covered with brown slime and lumps of the stuff covering her head and neck.

I stroked Mollie's face and ears and apologised for getting her into this mess. I was still trembling but she was remarkably calm and soon started to graze. I needed to pause and try to work things out with my map and compass. The valley ahead lay to the northeast, so the Valley of the Cows must be the one on the left. That was northwest, and I thought I could see a faint path traversing the shoulder toward it. In any case I had to get away from the bog, so retraced my steps and to my great relief soon came across hoof prints going in the right direction. My joy was short-lived; after a short distance I lost them again. Leaving Mollie to graze I set off on foot to reconnoitre but after a few yards realised that she was following me anxiously. There was nowhere to tie her; we had to do our path-seeking together. Using the compass to steer us, I led Mollie northwest. I managed to keep high and reasonably dry, skirting round the worst bits of bog and safely crossing a small river, until we came to a viewpoint and the discovery that I'd made a needless detour. The valley that I had rejected as being in the wrong direction at the end of the track was indeed the correct one. The old road was clearly and temptingly visible far below us as it followed the squiggling river along the broad valley to Castle Gregory, though its route down was hidden from view. But at least I knew where I was going; if I headed east across that flat grassy area I should pick up the path again. But it wasn't grass, it was bog.

Climbers and hikers dislike bog because of the discomfort of wet feet; there's little danger. But for a horse weighing a couple of hundredweight supported on pole-like legs, it's another matter. It was impossible to tell what was safe and what wasn't. Some wet areas looked lethal but afforded a firm footing, others looked almost dry and supported my weight but I would see Mollie go down. Time and again she sank above her hocks, struggling out before becoming more deeply bogged; but once she was again up to her belly, a pathetic legless figure with her chin resting on the ground and a look of defeat in her eyes. All I could do was urge her to make an effort, then watch helplessly as her struggles sank her deeper into the mire. I was as terrified that she'd pull a muscle as I was fearful that she would never get out. When she freed herself I hugged her in pride and gratitude and together we made our slow laborious way to the next viewpoint. When we reached it I shouted my relief. Not only were we out of the bogs, we were only about half a mile from the track. I could see it zigzagging up the far side of a deep canyon at the head of the valley, crossing the river near the top, then disappearing. I was perhaps 80 yards from where I'd lost the hoof-marked track.

Leaving Mollie tucking into the grass (it was now 5 o'clock and neither of us had had lunch) I started scouting out the best route and rearranging my night plans. I now doubted we'd get to Castle Gregory that day; better to camp in that lovely valley far below once we'd negotiated the switchbacks. There was plenty of grazing and we both deserved a good rest. But my musings were cut short. Between me and the track was the canyon, and I could see no way to reach the path running down its far side. Its steep sides were slick with rain, and grey rocks overhung the edge. To the north were more cliffs – not so steep – but deeper. The map showed an 800-foot drop to the valley; a person could probably make it down, I decided, but not a pony, and certainly not a laden pony. I felt close to despair. There was no choice but to cross that dreadful bog again to regain the high ground and retrace our steps. Returning to Mollie I told her without much conviction, to take heart, that it was nearly over. Taking the head collar I started to lead her back, but when she felt the soft ground beneath her feet, she made it clear that she would go no further. I mounted and urged her forward. We made reasonable progress, but with the extra weight she again went down, belly deep. This time she struggled free reasonably soon but one of her flailing hooves caught the back of my hand, which swelled alarmingly. I tried to get a grip on myself. Anxiety was making me careless; this was no place to risk a serious injury. But what could I do?

Then Mollie was down again. And this time she seemed ready to give up; she stayed immobile for what seemed like an eternity, breathing hard with the whites of her eyes showing. I knelt on the ground by her head, stroking her ears and talking, pleading and cajoling, I told her she must make one more effort, that we'd soon be all right. She turned her head and glanced back at the saddlebags. Of course! My earlier trembling had given way to a despairing calm and this time I was able to undo the buckles and remove the luggage. Mollie immediately renewed her struggle and managed to free herself. I knew then what I must do. There was no question of trying to reach the valley tonight – we were both nearly exhausted. I would set up my tent on the far side of the little river (the one that later plunged so frustratingly into the canyon) then try to persuade Mollie to join me. If only she could reach the river there was good grazing along the banks, and if I could find a ford, or a place where she could jump across, we'd be on the high heathery ground again with a clear route down to the valley.

Saddlebags are not designed to be carried and it took the last of my strength to heave them over the bogs and across stepping stones over the river. Dumping them on the firm ground on the opposite bank, I returned for Mollie. Without the bags surely I could lead her across that relatively short stretch of boggy ground. I'd worked out a moderately firm route but she resolutely refused to be led. When I got on her back she bravely took a step, sank, struggled out and stood firm. Nothing I could do, on or off, would move her. I took off the saddle and carried it across the bogs and the river. Then I set up the tent on the far bank. I needed time to think, but the only thought was that I *had* to get Mollie across the bog. She was standing on a little island of terra firma, and all around her was squelch.

Returning, I tried – whimpering in desperation – to lead her in every direction. I didn't care where she went as long as she got to solid ground. She stood firm with rolling eyes. My whimpers turned to sobs as I realised she was trembling. Overcome with remorse I pressed my forehead against her shoulder and wept. Mollie started nibbling at the scant grass. I took out her bit and went to the tent. I could see no way out. It was now 8 o'clock and with only three hours of daylight left I hardly had time to get help. And what sort of help could I get? Two wooden planks would do it – Mollie would walk along those to firm ground – or perhaps a roll of carpet. But they'd have to be carried up by hand; no tractor would get up to this place. And who would be willing to carry that sort of weight three or four miles and 800 feet up on a Saturday night? But I couldn't leave Mollie standing motionless all night, which she was apparently prepared to do. Horses keep warm by being constantly on the move. Black clouds were building up, rain was certain, and I was sure she'd catch a chill.

I did some fairly hard praying as I headed back to the Mollie Island. Having run out of options I just wanted some sort of divine solution. But when I reached the top of the hill my heart lurched in fear. She wasn't there. Had she tried to move and sunk into the bog again? But I couldn't see her white head. Then I raised my eyes and saw her calmly grazing on a firm grassy area on the far side of the marsh. She was safe! With a little cry of joy I floundered towards her and flung my arms round her neck. Now, at last, I could release all the desperate anxiety, guilt and loneliness of the last few hours in laughter and tears as I hugged and stroked her. We were all right. Together we had survived this dreadful day and tomorrow we would rest in Castle Gregory.

I spent the rest of the daylight hours devising a route from Mollie's grazing area to the firm ground where I had pitched my tent. The only potential problem seemed to be the river with marshy banks that separated her from this dry ground. From here I knew I that if I kept close to the cliffs I could stay on firm ground, and could now see where the path went, contouring the side of the cliff to cross the canyon where the river was shallow. We were so nearly there, the dangers were over and tomorrow we'd both be fresh. Mollie might baulk at crossing the river after her experiences of today, but if I left her untethered she would wander around keeping warm and regain her confidence. She could also make the most of the sparse grazing. I didn't think she'd go far.

The first drops of rain were falling as I climbed up the rise from the river to take a last look at my pony. She was standing watching me, ears pricked. "Good night Mollie!" I called out. As soon as I reached the tent the rain came crashing down, beaten against the flysheet by strong winds. I had little appetite but made a cup of tea. My companionable radio refused to work. I couldn't concentrate on a book, so I got into my sleeping bag and worried about Mollie, the terrible day that she'd had and now no shelter from the storm. But she was used to rain, I told myself; she'd just turn her back to the wind and wait it out.

Waking at 6.30 I ate my breakfast apple, teeth chattering against the morning cold as I pulled on sodden socks and boots. I'd have a proper breakfast once I'd retrieved Mollie. Putting the core in my pocket as a Good Morning present, I crossed the stream on the stepping stones and started to negotiate the bogs, stopping to admire a handsome red fox which trotted calmly across the cliff tops in front of me. I wasn't surprised to find that Mollie had wandered from her evening grazing area. From the many hoof prints beside the river I gathered that she'd paced backwards and forwards looking for a safe place to cross. There was certainly better grazing on the high ground near the cliffs. I couldn't tell if she'd succeeded in crossing so I trudged in large circles, expecting any minute to spot her in a dip or over the next rise. But nothing. Calling her name as I walked, I reached the cliff edge and looked down.

In the green valley far below I could see, along with the greyish dots of sheep, something larger and whiter. Why surely that was Mollie! The clever pony must have made her way down that perilously steep hill. But was it her? It could have been sunlight glinting on wet rocks. I went back to the tent for my binoculars. Yes, it was Mollie alright. . . but she was lying down. Well of course she'd be tired after the hard day and the effort of climbing down the cliff. Horses often sleep stretched out like that in the early morning. I called and whistled, expecting her to lift her head. No movement.

Fear gripped my heart as I started down the hill, slithering on the wet rocks, and lowering myself backwards down the steepest bits, grabbing handfuls of tussock grass. I was muttering over and over again, "Let it be all right. Oh please God make it all right." Halfway down I paused to check again with the binoculars, but not after that. I didn't want to see any more, I just wanted to believe that it was indeed all right, despite the mounting evidence: the smooth line of crushed grass showing the slide of a heavy body and the position she was lying in. I knew then what I would find. Mollie was dead.

I stared at her body. This couldn't be true. No, it wasn't Mollie, surely it was another horse! Then I looked at the hooves and the irrefutable evidence of the new shoes. I crouched down beside her and put my hand briefly on her shoulder, then turned away.

I climbed back up the cliff, devoid of all feeling, mechanically picking the safest route to my tent. Methodically I began the familiar process of breaking camp, stuffing my sleeping bag into its sack, removing the tent poles and folding up the tent. As I put the tent pegs in my pocket, I felt something: a plastic bag containing an apple core. Only then did I start to cry.

Chapter 14

It doesn't hit you at first, grief. Just as the body protects you from fully feeling the pain of an accident, so the mind stays clear of an emotional shock. I felt unreal, as though I was watching a video of me calmly getting on with the things that had to be done. I finished packing up the tent, organised the saddlebags, and put the saddle and tack into a bin liner tied up with the reins. I carried the bags, one at a time, across the river, through the bogs and up to the cliff top, resolutely keeping my mind in the present. I dropped the bag with the saddle and tack down the cliff and watched it bounce out of sight. Then I climbed down with the strap of the saddlebags wound around my fingers, tightening with each rotation of the dangling bag. I was deliberately reckless, knowing that I'd be unable to release my fingers should I, or the bag, slip and gather momentum. The only thing that mattered was to steer my thoughts away from what I'd seen at the bottom of the cliff. For Mollie was not only dead, but horribly dead. The foxes had reached her first and started to feast on her soft body.

Dragging the saddlebags across the last flat stretch I propped them against a stone wall and returned to look for the grey bag containing the saddle. Eventually I had to admit defeat. It had completely disappeared and

I was nearing the end of my strength. Someone would have to help me carry the saddlebags to the road, and later I would go back and find the saddle.

I waded across the river and started walking down the track I'd seen from the cliffs. After about a mile I heard a whistle and saw a shepherd with his dog. As always when approaching a stranger, I mentally prepared my opening request, but all that came out was a sob. I couldn't talk about what had happened. The poor man was at a loss to know what to do. He put his hand on my sodden trousers. "But y're soaked to the skin!"

"No, no, it's my horse... I need help to get the bags..."

He couldn't understand me. "My horse is *dead*!" He still couldn't get it. Plenty of walkers come that way, but not horses. He looked perplexed and told me he was searching for a lamb, but he followed me to the saddlebags and I pointed to Mollie. Then he understood. Or he understood the fact, not the emotion. What I needed most was cheering up. As we shouldered the saddlebags between us he started a lively conversation, beginning "I'm after considering how old ye might be." After that subject was exhausted he went on to discuss my marital status, past and present, the problems of marriage, divorce in Ireland, bronchitis and how to cure it, lambs, sheep and sheep dogs. Did I earn a lot of money? Did I do manual work (looking at my broken nails and grime-engrained hands). It worked, I allowed myself to be distracted, I felt stronger and I was able to explain about the missing saddle.

Eamonn's protective instincts were now in full flow. He was not going to allow me to climb that cliff again. Nor was he going to climb that cliff. He told me of a young man who'd been killed at that very spot a few years earlier. A lovely boy he was, the eldest son.

Eamonn and I carried the saddlebag between us. Sometimes we hugged it across our front; sometimes we humped it over our shoulders. We rested often. I had sunk into a dreamy state of deep fatigue, answering his cheerful questions automatically. Then we saw another figure high on the hill. "Noel!

There's a tourist here with a dead horse! Are you going into the hills or are you going home?" Not surprisingly Noel was no quicker on the uptake than Eamonn had been. I could only understand one word of his answer. It began with F. "Never mind, let's just carry on!" I muttered. "Oh, don't you mind him. His bark's worse than his bite. "Noel, are you going into the hills. . .?" After what seemed like an age, Noel came down from the mountainside. A thin-faced, intelligent-looking young man of few words, he took stock of the problem, lifted up the bag and strode off down the path. We soon reached the road; Eamonn disappeared home (I didn't even have the chance to thank him) and Noel marched through the front door of the house opposite and dumped my bags without a word on the sofa.

The Hennessy family were watching Ronald Reagan on TV. All turned around with one movement and looked at me open-mouthed. Once my presence was explained I was given a chair by the fire. I peeled off my wet things, took off my sodden boots and socks, and sat like a zombie while Ronnie droned on in Ballyporeen. Tea arrived, then a meal (my first in 24 hours) and I began to feel better. In the late afternoon another son arrived and he and Noel discussed going back up the track to look for the saddle. I said I'd come but had a more pressing matter on my mind. "Can we bury the pony?" I asked. "I don't want to just leave her there. I can't just leave her there!" I started to cry again. The boys glanced at each other. "Don't worry, we'll deal with it."

I followed them up the track, wiping the tears from my face with the back of my hand and trying to make some decisions. Without Mollie I couldn't finish my trip. But I couldn't imagine summoning the necessary energy to carry all my gear back to London. Noel's mother, Kathleen, had invited me to spend the night and helped me move my stuff into the spare room. No need to think about anything today – except finding that damned saddle. It was Mollie's; I had to get it back. The two boys were nearly at the top of the cliff when I got there, but they'd found nothing. I searched fruitlessly for nearly an hour, resolutely keeping away from Mollie's body. It was after I'd given up in the renewed rain that I saw the bag, resting against a boulder in one of the streams that ran down the mountain. It was good to have something to be pleased about.

Back at the house the TV coverage of Reagan's visit was over, and the family conversation was in full flight. Noel and Paddy were men of few words but Kathleen had plenty to say. She was filled with admiration at my sleeping alone on the mountains.

"Dear Lord! I'm telling you, girlie, I wouldn't go there for all the tea in China!"

When her husband was alive they had lived along the track leading to the mountains. Indeed, she'd been born there in the little house whose ruins I'd seen at the junction of two rivers cascading down the cliffs. Everyone, she said, knew about the Thing that had haunted the valley about 80 years ago. It was like a huge barrel and it rolled around, up and down the hills and sometimes over the roofs of the houses, making a sound that was half-man, half-goat. Her father-in-law's cowman was once chased by the Thing and took refuge in the cowshed where he was trapped for three hours. In the end they asked the priest to perform an exorcism ceremony, and the Thing no longer bothered anyone in the house.

"Ooh Jesus, you'd never find me sleeping in those mountains. Here's another story. When I was a girl I went up the valley after our cows. And there was a large black bullock lying down. Huge, it was. Bigger than any of our animals and I didn't recognise it as belonging to any of the neighbours. I'd never seen it before. So I collected our own animals and I kept looking at this bullock and wondering about it, and I watched it get to its feet. I turned away for a minute and when I looked again it had disappeared. I never saw it again. I was that frightened; I ran all the way home."

Something had made Mollie try to descend the cliff. Or did she fall from the top? Did she lose her footing in the darkness or was she trying to escape from the storm? Was she looking for me or seeking better grazing in the valley? Or had something so frightened her that this sure-footed and sensible pony, born and bred in the Connemara mountains, the Mollie who'd always known what actions were safe and who just wouldn't allow me to do anything dangerous, had become reckless? I'll never know.

The talk of ghosts continued. Kathleen's husband, Mick, now dead, a phlegmatic practical sort of chap, had seen a tall man standing by a gate. But he wasn't just tall he was 10-feet tall or so, and he wasn't by the gate, he was part of it... Mick fled, but was convinced that he'd seen his dead father. By this time it was dark, but no-one turned on the lights. Suddenly, behind me, I was aware of a very tall man standing silently in the doorway. I gasped. "Jack!" said Kathleen. Jack came in and talked. And talked. He was angry about something and the family were falling about with laughter. I couldn't laugh because I couldn't understand a word he said. "This is my niece from England," said Kathleen, giving me an elaborate wink. Jack was a frequent visitor, I was told afterwards. He often stayed late into the night because he was afraid of going home in the dark and was known for his insatiable curiosity. One ear was keyhole shaped, they claimed. He'd once been disturbed kneeling outside the door while a family argument was taking place. "Why I was just saying a prayer for Mick, God rest his soul."

"Time you were away, Jack, it's getting very dark." Jack reluctantly left and I was shown to the spare room. I got into bed, put the pillow over my head and sobbed.

Next morning I made some decisions. I would go back to England but leave my gear at the Hennessy's and try to hire another pony once I felt ready. The Hennessys encouraged this plan; they knew someone who could fix me up with a suitable animal. One of the boys gave me a lift into Tralee. It was

Whit Monday and raining. The shops were closed and the place deserted except for clusters of young people looking for fun. I trailed dejectedly round, filling in time before the bus left. It was packed with cheerful youngsters, which increased my gloom.

Six hours to Dublin. It was too long, too much time for reflection. I tried to read but instead of the words I saw Mollie's outstretched body. I looked out of the window at the lovely translucent green of the evening fields and scowled at their beauty. A white horse was grazing near the road and my tears started again. I couldn't stop thinking about her; I recalled the shape of her ears as seen from the saddle, the pink diamond on her nose, her little moustache, her dark brown eyes with white eyelashes, her abundant mane and the feeling of the soft folds of skin between her front legs. I remember the slap I used to give her bottom as I moved round her, grooming or saddling up, and of course her little gestures of affection.

The 'if only's' churned endlessly round in my mind. If only I'd been more careful in following the hoof prints; if only I'd turned back after the first bogging; if only I'd moved the tent to where Mollie was spending the night; if only I'd tethered her. Relentlessly I relived every moment, imagining the things I should have done, inventing dozens of plausible happy endings. But I had thought I had a happy ending when Mollie got clear of her island. After that elation how could fate deal me such a blow? In my worst imaginings, such an end had never occurred to me. If only. . .

Epilogue: Peggy

I returned to Castle Gregory in August and continued the ride with Peggy, eventually clocking up a total of a thousand miles. And that story has a happy ending.

Dingle Peggy will be published in 2013.